Science

FOR COMMON ENTRANCE

13+

Revision Guide

Richard Balding

GALORE PARK

AN HACHETTE UK COMPANY

About the author

Richard Balding has wide experience of teaching science in prep schools, culminating in 26 years running the science department at Summer Fields. During his career, he has been the IAPS science coordinator, chairman of the Physics Common Entrance setting panel and SATIPS broadsheet editor, and was a marker for Key Stage 3 SATS. Publications include books on physics, chemistry and biology, written for prep schools. Now retired from teaching, he is active as an ISI inspector, writing and editing science books.

Acknowledgements

I would like to dedicate this book to all pupils who are working towards a sound knowledge of science, which will also enable them to achieve well in the Common Entrance exam. I would also like to thank all my past pupils for making the journey so enjoyable, and colleagues from many common rooms for help, support and guidance over the years. Finally, thanks must go to the editorial and production teams at Galore Park for the publication of this guide, which I hope continues to be of help to those who use it.

Every effort has been made to trace all copyright holders, but if any have been inadvertently overlooked, the Publishers will be pleased to make the necessary arrangements at the first opportunity.

Although every effort has been made to ensure that website addresses are correct at time of going to press, Galore Park cannot be held responsible for the content of any website mentioned in this book. It is sometimes possible to find a relocated web page by typing in the address of the home page for a website in the URL window of your browser.

Hachette UK's policy is to use papers that are natural, renewable and recyclable products and made from wood grown in sustainable forests. The logging and manufacturing processes are expected to conform to the environmental regulations of the country of origin.

Orders: please contact Bookpoint Ltd, 130 Park Drive, Milton Park, Abingdon, Oxon OX14 4SE. Telephone: (44) 01235 827720. Fax: (44) 01235 400454. Email education@bookpoint.co.uk Lines are open from 9 a.m. to 5 p.m., Monday to Saturday, with a 24-hour message answering service. Visit our website at www.galorepark.co.uk for details of other revision guides for Common Entrance, examination papers and Galore Park publications.

ISBN: 978 1 4718 4716 5

© Richard Balding 2015

First published in 2015 by

Galore Park Publishing Ltd,

An Hachette UK Company

Carmelite House

50 Victoria Embankment

London EC4Y 0DZ

www.galorepark.co.uk

Impression number   10 9 8 7 6 5 4

Year   2019 2018 2017

The following illustrations are by Aptara, Inc.: p5(t), p5(b), p8(t), p8(b), p9, p11, p13, p17, p18, p25, p29, p32, p36, p37, p38, p40, p41, p45(t), p45(b), p46, p55(t), p55(b), p56, p58(t), p58(b), p66, p71, p74, p79, p91, p93, p94, p97(t), p97(b), p107, p110, p112, p116(t), p116(b), p117(t), p117(b), p120(t), p120(b), p121, p131(t), p131(b), p133, p135, p144, p146, p151

All other illustrations are by Ian Moores and are reused with permission.

Typeset in India by Aptara, Inc.

Printed in India

A catalogue record for this title is available from the British Library.

Contents

Introduction

This book will help you to produce your best in the Common Entrance examination at 13+. As well as working carefully through your course, you will need to do some revision, especially as it may be 2 years or more since you studied some of the early topics. As this book is a revision guide, it contains only an outline of the topics that will be examined; fuller treatment of these will be found in *Science for Common Entrance: Biology*, *Science for Common Entrance: Chemistry* and *Science for Common Entrance: Physics*. To find out whether you know and understand the key facts within each topic, each section includes a selection of questions so that you can familiarise yourself with what you might expect to see in the exam.

In the 13+ examination, questions will be set that will assume a thorough knowledge of the topics covered in the sections we have called 'Make sure you know'. These sections cover the material required for the 11+ exam. It is always a good idea to read through the 11+ materials on the topic you are revising. In most cases you will be refreshing what you know already, so this will be a relatively small but worthwhile task.

The syllabus and your examinations

To help you in planning your revision, it is useful to know about the syllabus used for the exam.

This is revised regularly and is based on the programme of study for Key Stage 2 (11+) and Key Stage 3 (13+) of the National Curriculum for Science. Because Key Stage 3 covers years 7–9, the Common Entrance syllabus does not include all Key Stage 3 topics; many of these will be taught at senior school level.

Working scientifically

The exam will be based on the key concepts, skills and processes that you need to experience to deepen and broaden your understanding of science. These are listed below.

Scientific attitudes

Candidates are expected to:

- pay attention to objectivity and concern for accuracy, precision, repeatability and reproducibility
- understand that scientific methods and theories develop as scientists modify earlier explanations to take account of new evidence and ideas
- learn to evaluate risks
- understand the power and limitations of science and potential ethical questions and debates
- consider the validity of experimental results in terms of fair testing.

Experimental skills and investigations

Candidates are expected to:

- ask questions and develop a line of enquiry based on observations of the real world, alongside prior knowledge and experience

- make predictions using scientific knowledge and understanding

- select, plan and carry out the most appropriate types of scientific enquiries to test predictions, including identifying independent, dependent and control variables, where appropriate

- use appropriate techniques, apparatus and materials during fieldwork and laboratory work, paying attention to health and safety

- make and record observations and measurements using a range of methods for different investigations; evaluate the reliability of methods and suggest possible improvements or further investigations

- apply sampling techniques

- use scientific theories, models and explanations to develop hypotheses

- plan investigations to make observations and to test hypotheses, including identifying variables as independent, dependent or control, and measure and consider other factors that need to be taken into account when collecting evidence

- measure and manipulate concentrations.

Analysis, evaluation and problem-solving

Candidates are expected to:

- apply mathematical concepts and calculate results

- undertake basic data analysis, including statistical techniques

- use and derive simple equations and carry out appropriate calculations

- present observations and data, using appropriate methods, including tables and graphs; carry out and represent mathematical and simple statistical analysis

- interpret observations and data, including identifying patterns and using observations, measurements and data to draw conclusions

- present reasoned explanations, including explaining data in relation to predictions and hypotheses

- evaluate data, showing awareness of potential sources of random and systematic error

- identify further questions arising from their results

- represent random distribution of results and estimate uncertainty; interpret observations and data, including identifying patterns and trends, and use observations, measurements and data to make inferences and draw conclusions

- evaluate data critically, showing awareness of potential sources of random variations and systematic errors, and suggest improvements

- communicate the scientific rationale for the investigation and the methods used, giving accounts of findings, reasoned explanation of data in relation to hypotheses and reasoned conclusions through written reports and electronic presentations.

Measurement

Candidates are expected to:

● understand and use SI units and IUPAC (International Union of Pure and Applied Chemistry) chemical nomenclature

● convert units.

Your exams at 13+

Assessment of the 13+ syllabus can occur at two levels: Level 1 and Level 2. The syllabus is common for both levels. It is envisaged that candidates who are expected to achieve less than an average of 40% on the three Level 2 papers should consider using the Level 1 paper.

Level 1 (80 marks; 60 minutes)

There will be one paper with approximately equal numbers of questions based on the 13+ biology, chemistry and physics syllabuses. The paper will consist of a mixture of closed items, for example multiple choice, matching pairs, completing sentences and some open questions. Open questions will have several parts, some of which will require answers of one or two sentences. These parts will carry a maximum of 3 marks. At least 25% of the paper will be testing *Working Scientifically*.

For questions that require the use of formulae, equations will be provided. Rearrangement of equations will not be required.

There will be no choice of questions. The use of calculators and protractors will be allowed in the examination.

Level 2 (60 marks; 40 minutes)

There will be three papers, one in each of biology, chemistry and physics. Some of the questions may be closed, although most will be open with several parts requiring candidates to answer in sentences. These parts will carry a maximum of 4 marks. In addition, 1 mark may be given for an acceptable standard of spelling, punctuation and grammar in one part of the paper. The maximum number of marks per question will be 12. At least 25% of the paper will be testing *Working Scientifically*

There will be no choice of questions. The use of calculators and protractors will be allowed in the examination.

For quantitative questions that require the use of formulae, equations given in the syllabus will *not* be provided.

Scholarship

Scholarship papers are based on this syllabus. The Common Academic Scholarship Examination (90 minutes, including 10 minutes' reading time) will be divided into three sections: A (Biology), B (Chemistry) and C (Physics). Candidates will be required to attempt all questions. Each section is worth 25 marks but the number of questions will vary. The use of calculators and protractors will be allowed in the examination.

For quantitative questions that require the use of formulae, equations given in the syllabus will *not* be provided. Rearrangement of equations may be required.

Tips on revising

Get the best out of your brain

- Give your brain plenty of oxygen by exercising. You can revise effectively if you feel fit and well.

- Eat healthy food while you are revising. Your brain works better when you give it good fuel.

- Think *positively*. Give your brain positive messages so that it will want to study.

- Keep calm. If your brain is stressed it will not operate effectively.

- Take regular breaks during your study time.

- Get enough sleep. Your brain will carry on sorting out what you have revised while you sleep.

Get the most from your revision

- Don't work for hours without a break. Revise for 20–30 minutes, then take a 5-minute break.

- Do good things in your breaks: listen to your favourite music, eat healthy food, drink some water, do some exercise and juggle. Don't read a book, watch TV or play on the computer – it will conflict with what your brain is trying to learn.

- When you go back to your revision review what you have just learnt.

- Regularly review the facts you have learnt.

Get motivated

- Set yourself some goals and promise yourself a treat when the exams are over.

- Make the most of all the expertise and talent available to you at school and at home. If you don't understand something ask your teacher to explain.

- Get organised. Find a quiet place to revise and make sure you have all the equipment you need.

Know what to expect in the examination

- Use past papers to familiarise yourself with the format of the exam.

- Make sure you understand the language examiners use.

Before the examination

- Have all your equipment and pens ready the night before.

- Make sure you are at your best by getting a good night's sleep before the exam.

- Have a good breakfast in the morning.

- Take some water into the exam if you are allowed.

- Think positively and keep calm.

During the examination

- Have a watch on your desk. Work out how much time you need to allocate to each question and try to stick to it.

- Make sure you read and understand the instructions and rules on the front of the exam paper.

- Allow some time at the start to read and consider the questions carefully before writing anything.

- Read all the questions at least twice. Don't rush into answering before you have a chance to think about it.

- If a question is particularly hard move on to the next one. Go back to it if you have time at the end.

- Always look on the back of the paper because there might be questions there that you have not answered.

- Check your answers make sense if you have time at the end.

Tips for the science examination

- You should write your answers on the question paper.

- You may use a calculator.

- Remember that *all* questions should be attempted.

- Look at the number of marks allocated for each question in order to assess how many relevant points are required for a full answer. Very often, marks are awarded for giving your reasons for writing a particular answer.

- In numerical questions, workings out should be shown and the correct units used.

- Practical skills are important. Look back in your lab notes to remind yourself about why you carried out any practical work. What were you trying to find out? What did you actually do? What instrument did you use to take any measurements and what units did you use? How did you record your results: tables, bar charts or graphs? What were the results of your investigation and did you make any plans to change or improve what you did? These are all important and will be tested in the examination.

- A thorough understanding of your practical work will also help you to remember the key facts by putting them into context.

- Neat handwriting and careful presentation may help to put the examiner in a more generous frame of mind!

1 Preliminary knowledge for 13+ Biology

→ **Revision tip**

This chapter is divided into four sections and contains material you MUST KNOW to be successful at 13+ exams.

Be sure that you can answer ALL the questions in this chapter as a first part of your revision.

1.1 Life processes

What is a living thing?

A living thing is called an organism.

This term will apply to any living thing, whether it is the smallest bacterium or the tallest tree.

While there are huge numbers of different organisms, there will be processes that they carry out that are shared by each and every one of them in order that they may be classified as living. These are called life processes – sometimes called characteristics of living.

There are seven of these processes but by now you will only be required to know four of them.

1 Nutrition

Just as car engines require fuel to make them work, so all organisms need to be able to obtain and absorb food that provides them with energy to live and materials to help build up and maintain their bodies.

- Animals: food needs to be broken down by the process called digestion, so that they can use the different types of chemical in the food in various ways.
- Plants: the process is less obvious, but you will know that plants die if they are starved of water and that they need certain minerals to achieve healthy **growth**.

2 Movement

- Animals: this is obvious as they will move from place to place to find food, or escape from being someone else's food. They will move to find a mate, shelter, or to escape natural disasters such as floods or forest fires.
- Plants: movement is so slow that it cannot be seen with the naked eye. Petals will open and close and whole **flower** heads will turn following the path of the sun. **Shoots** respond to **light** and **roots** to **gravity**. Even though they have moved, you will not have been able to detect the slow movement.

3 Reproduction

All organisms need to reproduce.

As each individual organism, sooner or later, will die, it is vital that it is able to make more of its own kind so that there is continuity of that type of organism.

This is the way in which features (called **characteristics**) are carried forward from parents to the next generation (called **offspring**).

4 Growth

All organisms are made up from individual building blocks called **cells**.

Growth is how an organism becomes bigger and sometimes more complicated.

The organs in animals and plants that carry out the life processes
An **organ** is a structure that performs a particular function.

Organs in plants

- Flower: its main function is to make **seeds** and the flower will contain the reproductive organs. Each seed will, with successful **germination**, grow into a new plant. Some flowers rely upon being visited by insects to help with **reproduction**. In order to attract insects, the flower will either put on an attractive display (colour and shape of petals), or produce a distinctive smell (scent), or both.

- Leaves: each **leaf** is a miniature factory, making the food that the plant needs in order for it to grow. The large, flat surfaces, together with the green colour (**chlorophyll**), trap the light needed for the plant to make food by the process called **photosynthesis**.

- Photosynthesis is the name given to the method plants use to make food to feed themselves: photo (= light); synthesis (= making).

- **Stem**: this does two important jobs – support and transport:
  - Support: flowers need to be displayed to attract insects for reproduction; leaves need to be held up to the light.
  - Transport: the stem contains various tubes that: move water and minerals from the roots to all parts of the plant; move food produced in the leaves to the growing and storage places.

- Roots: the root system has two main jobs to do:
  - To hold the plant firmly in the soil.
  - To absorb water and minerals from the soil through tiny root hairs on the outside of the roots, which increase the surface area for better absorption of water and minerals such as nitrates.

Organs in animals

- **Brain**: this receives messages from all parts of the body through the nervous system (a network of nerves connected to the brain by the spinal cord). The information in these messages is received and instructions are sent to control the life processes of movement, nutrition, reproduction and growth.

- **Lungs:** they take oxygen from the air and pass it into our blood and at the same time remove waste carbon dioxide from our blood and pass it into the air. This is known as gaseous exchange and the lung surface is folded greatly creating a large surface area to achieve this. Smoking reduces this surface area, leading to severe breathing difficulties and, often, serious disease.

- **Heart:** this pumps the blood, which carries digested food, oxygen and waste products to and from all parts of the body. The flow of blood needs to happen continuously to maintain life and the heart is the pump that makes this happen.

- **Stomach:** here food is mixed with chemicals as part of the digestive process.

- **Intestines:** a long tube where digested food is absorbed into the bloodstream and solid waste is collected to be egested through the anus.

- **Liver:** many chemical reactions take place here and digested food from the intestine is treated and sent to the part of the body where it is needed.

- **Kidneys:** soluble waste is filtered out here, is collected in the bladder and removed from the body in the form of urine.

Adaptation

Features of organisms that fit them to their surroundings and increase their chances of survival

Domestic pets and farm animals are provided with food and shelter. This is not so for animals that live in the wild and they will have features, for example sharp claws and good eyesight, that will enable them to survive. Plants will also develop in different ways to be able to grow in different conditions.

 Revision tip

Use the glossary at the back of the book for definitions of key words.

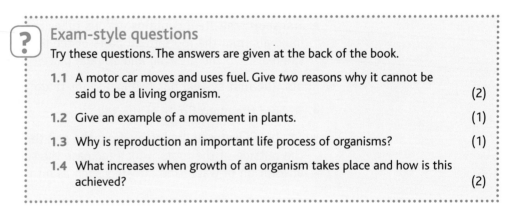

? Exam-style questions

Try these questions. The answers are given at the back of the book.

1.1 A motor car moves and uses fuel. Give *two* reasons why it cannot be said to be a living organism. (2)

1.2 Give an example of a movement in plants. (1)

1.3 Why is reproduction an important life process of organisms? (1)

1.4 What increases when growth of an organism takes place and how is this achieved? (2)

1.5 For the diagram below, match each of the following organs to its numbered label:

flower   stem   root   leaf   (4)

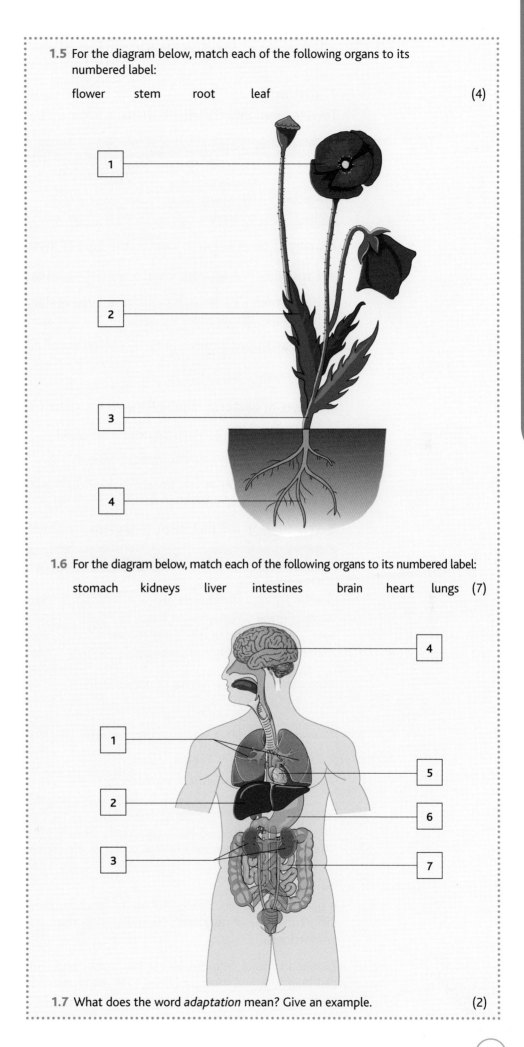

1.6 For the diagram below, match each of the following organs to its numbered label:

stomach   kidneys   liver   intestines   brain   heart   lungs   (7)

1.7 What does the word *adaptation* mean? Give an example.   (2)

1.2 Humans and other animals

Nutrition

Food is taken into the mouth where it is cut up by teeth.

Type of tooth	Shape	Function
Canine	Pointed	Tear food – killing
Incisor	Sharp-edged chisel	Cut food
Pre-molar	Two pointed ridges	Tear and grind food
Molar	Broad ridges	Grind and crush food

Looking at teeth helps to identify the type of diet.

- **Carnivores** – meat eaters will have large **canines** and **incisors**.

- **Herbivores** – plant eaters will have large **molars** and **pre-molars** but may have small canines and incisors.

- Meat and plant eaters will have a selection of all four types of teeth.

Care of teeth:

- A layer of **bacteria** called **plaque** turns sugar from food into acid.

- Acid attacks the enamel, causing tooth decay.

- Regular brushing helps to remove plaque.

- Fluoride in water or toothpaste makes tooth enamel harder and more resistant to acid attack.

- Less sugar in the diet helps to prevent tooth decay.

Type of food	Where found	How it is used
Carbohydrates:		
Starches	Bread, pasta, rice	Supply of energy
Sugars (glucose)	Cakes, sweets, fruit	Supply of energy
Fats	Meat, milk, butter, cheese	Store of energy, insulation
Proteins	Fish, meat, milk, eggs	Manufacture, growth and repair of cells
Mineral salts	Meat, vegetables, dairy products	Calcium – needed to form healthy bones Iron – needed to make red blood cells
Vitamins*	Fruit, vegetables, dairy products	Make certain chemical reactions happen that keep the body free from disease
Fibre	Cereals, fruit, vegetables	Helps passage of food through the digestive system
Water	Drinks, some foods (salads)	Dissolves and transports materials

*Vitamins such as vitamin C are not produced by the body, so have to be taken in by food. Lack of vitamin C causes bleeding gums (scurvy), poor growth in children and very slow tissue repair.

Balanced diet

A balanced diet includes a mixture of foods to provide us with all the different types of **nutrients** (listed above) that we need, in the correct proportions.

We need to take care not to eat too much food containing animal fat as this can lead to circulation problems that could result in heart disease.

Biology

Circulation

- Oxygen enters the body through the lungs and into the blood.

- The heart pumps blood to all cells in **arteries**.

- Oxygen and food are carried to all cells in the blood so that the energy needed for all life processes can be released by a process called **respiration**.

- Carbon dioxide and waste materials return to the heart in **veins**.

- Blood is pumped to the lungs where carbon dioxide leaves the body.

- The heart pumps blood through a contraction of the heart muscle (known as a heartbeat or **pulse**). Normal pulse rate is about 70 beats per minute.

- Exercise means that more food and oxygen are needed by the cells so the heart beats faster to achieve this.

Look up the experiment you did when you measured your heartbeat at rest, then again after exercise. You will remember that there was a big difference as the heart had to supply more oxygen to the cells to release more energy quickly because energy was being used during the exercise.

Did you record how long after exercise the heart took to return to normal ('at rest') heartbeat?

Benefits of exercise

- Heart muscle is in better shape because of regular use, reducing risk of heart attack.

- Excess carbohydrate and fat is used up, reducing **obesity**.

- Body muscles are in better shape, increasing ability to exercise for longer (**stamina**).

How we move
Humans are **vertebrates** and have an internal skeleton made of bones that:

- supports the body

- protects the brain (skull) and nerve cord (backbone or vertebral column)

- allows movement (muscles will move those bones where there are joints).

They are called vertebrates because they have a backbone (vertebral column) that protects the spinal nerve cord.

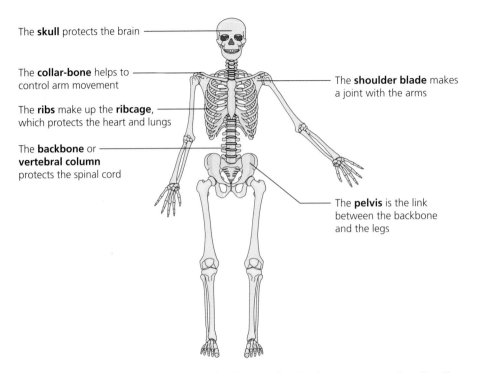

The **skull** protects the brain

The **collar-bone** helps to control arm movement

The **ribs** make up the **ribcage**, which protects the heart and lungs

The **backbone** or **vertebral column** protects the spinal cord

The **shoulder blade** makes a joint with the arms

The **pelvis** is the link between the backbone and the legs

There are just over 200 bones in the human body. Bones are made of cells located within layers of calcium phosphate (a hard material). In the centre of the bone is the bone marrow where new bone cells (and red blood cells) are formed.

Leg bones, which have to support the whole body, are much larger than the arm bones. Arms and legs move because the bones are levers that pivot about joints (synovial joints).

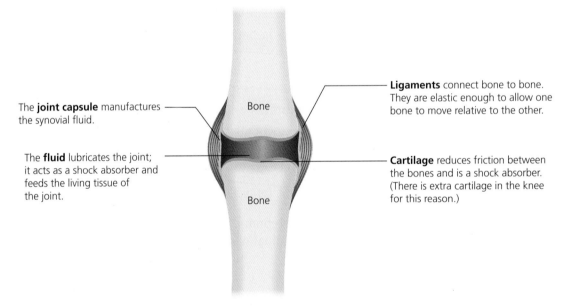

The **joint capsule** manufactures the synovial fluid.

The **fluid** lubricates the joint; it acts as a shock absorber and feeds the living tissue of the joint.

Bone

Bone

Ligaments connect bone to bone. They are elastic enough to allow one bone to move relative to the other.

Cartilage reduces friction between the bones and is a shock absorber. (There is extra cartilage in the knee for this reason.)

■ Synovial joint

How are bones able to move?

● This is achieved by the action of opposing (antagonistic) pairs of muscles.

● Muscle fibres shorten (contract) when a signal is received from the nervous system.

● When muscle action is no longer required, the muscle relaxes and goes back to its original length.

Muscles can only contract – they never push.

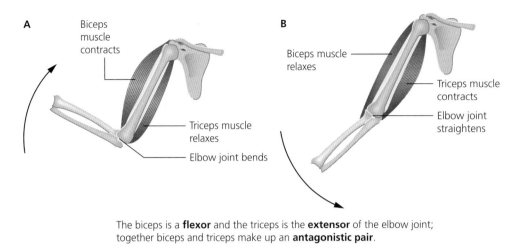

A Biceps muscle contracts

Triceps muscle relaxes

Elbow joint bends

B Biceps muscle relaxes

Triceps muscle contracts

Elbow joint straightens

The biceps is a **flexor** and the triceps is the **extensor** of the elbow joint; together biceps and triceps make up an **antagonistic pair**.

■ **A**. Action of the biceps muscle bending; **B**. Action of the triceps muscle

Stages in human growth and development

- Fertilised egg: the joining of special cells from the mother and the father.
- Embryo: development of the new human inside the mother.
- Baby: cannot feed or walk without help.
- Child: can feed, walk and talk but is still reliant on help from parents.
- Adolescent: sex organs mature but growth continues.
- Adult: growth complete; reproduction is possible.
- Old age: no growth; some life processes work less well.
- Death: life processes come to a stop.

Healthy living

As well as having a balanced diet and taking regular exercise, it is important not to put our bodies at risk from the following:

- Smoking tobacco: risk of lung cancer, heart attack, difficult breathing.
- Alcohol: risk of damage to liver, stomach and heart.
- Solvents and aerosols: risk of damage to brain and suffocation.
- Drugs: risk of damage to many life processes and may damage the brain, liver and stomach.

Microorganisms that cause disease in humans

There are two main types:

- **Viruses**, which are simple organisms that do not contain the chemical structures to enable them to reproduce, so they need to invade a living cell to achieve this. Because they live in a host cell and often do harm to the organism in which they live, it is very difficult to kill the virus without harming the host cell. Ebola, AIDS and various types of influenza are examples of diseases caused by viruses.

- **Bacteria**, which can live and grow outside living cells and when conditions are right can reproduce very quickly. Medicines in the form of antibiotics can kill bacteria. The first antibiotic was discovered in 1928 by Alexander Fleming, who discovered penicillin. Cholera and various types of food poisoning are caused by bacteria.

? Exam-style questions

Try these questions. The answers are given at the back of the book.

1.8 Make a table with the left-hand column listing the four main kinds of teeth. Fill in the right-hand column with the correct function of each type of tooth. (8)

1.9 (a) What causes tooth decay? (1)

(b) List three things that you can do to prevent tooth decay. (3)

1.10 Why will taking exercise cause the heart to beat faster? (2)

1.11 An athlete's pulse was taken three times:

A   just before a race

B   immediately after the race

C   10 minutes after the race.

How would you expect the pulse rate to change:

(a) between tests A and B? (1)

(b) between tests B and C? (2)

1.12 What are the three functions of a skeleton?

1.13 Suggest why the following two gases are important to plants:

(a) oxygen (1)

(b) carbon dioxide. (1)

1.14 Complete the table to show why the following factors are important in healthy plant growth. (5)

Factor	Why the factor is important to healthy plant growth
Air	
Light	
Warmth	
Water	
Minerals	

1.15 (a) Why are muscles that are used for controlled movement at a joint found in pairs? (2)

(b) Give an example of one pair. (1)

(c) What is the general name given to the type of paired muscles in (b)? (1)

1.16 What is the function of the following skeletal structures?

(a) Skull (1)

(b) Vertebrae (backbone) (1)

(c) Ribs (1)

1.3 Variation and classification

Diagnostic features

The differences between living organisms within a species are called variations. We use the diagnostic features of organisms to produce keys.

Spider or branching key

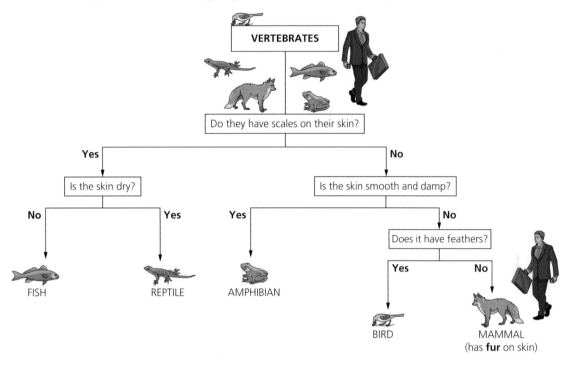

Number key

1	Do they have scales on their skin?
	YES Go to question 2
	NO Go to question 3
2	Is the skin dry?
	YES Reptile
	NO Fish
3	Is the skin smooth and damp?
	YES Amphibian
	NO Go to question 4
4	Does it have feathers?
	YES Bird
	NO Mammal

Remember that some features of organisms – e.g. type of skin in vertebrates – help you to sort them into groups whereas features such as size or weight do not.

Classification

Sorting organisms into groups is called classification. Organisms are given Latin names, which identifies them within particular groups largely as a result of the pioneering work carried out in this field by Carl Linnaeus.

The largest groups are kingdoms, e.g. plant kingdom, animal kingdom. Kingdoms are divided into groups.

The animal kingdom

Animals fall into two main groups:

- Vertebrates – animals have a backbone and an internal skeleton, made of bone.
- Invertebrates – animals do not have a backbone or a skeleton made of bone.

Arthropods are one of the sub-groups of **invertebrates**. All animals in this group have:

- jointed limbs (arthro = jointed; poda = limbs)
- hard outer body covering
- segmented bodies.

The group is divided into classes. Two of the classes are insects and arachnids.

Class	Number of body parts	Number of legs	Antennae	Wings	Typical examples
Insects	3	6	Yes	Yes	Bee, fly, beetle
Arachnids	2	8	No	No	Tarantula, scorpion, mite, tick

The plant kingdom

All plants within this kingdom make their own food by the process of photosynthesis.

There are four main groups of plants within the plant kingdom.

Group	Leaves	Stem	Root	Flower
Algae (e.g. seaweed)	–	–	–	–
Mosses	Simple	Yes	Yes	–
Ferns	Yes	–	Yes	–
Flowering plants (produce seeds)	Yes	Yes	Yes	Yes

Fungi are in a separate kingdom because they do not contain chlorophyll, do not carry out photosynthesis and obtain their food from their surroundings.

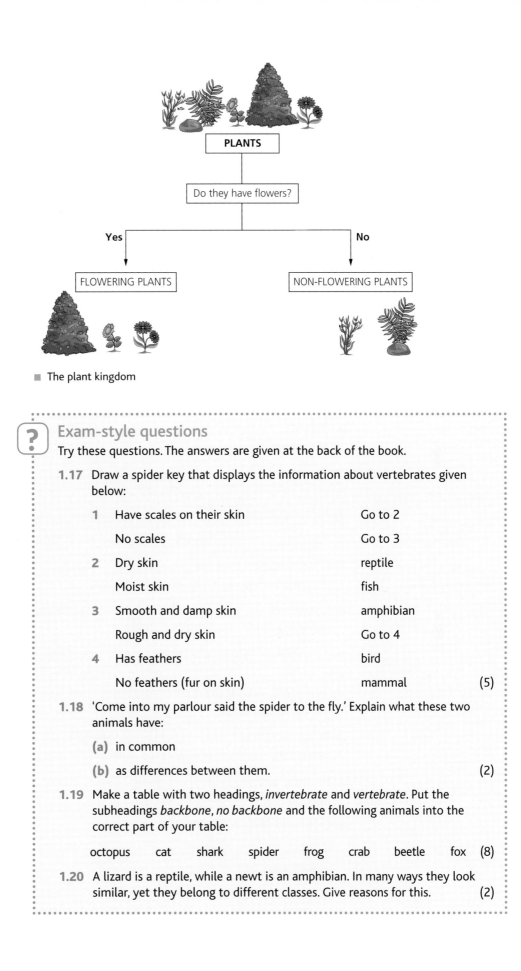

The plant kingdom

Exam-style questions

Try these questions. The answers are given at the back of the book.

1.17 Draw a spider key that displays the information about vertebrates given below:

1	Have scales on their skin	Go to 2
	No scales	Go to 3
2	Dry skin	reptile
	Moist skin	fish
3	Smooth and damp skin	amphibian
	Rough and dry skin	Go to 4
4	Has feathers	bird
	No feathers (fur on skin)	mammal (5)

1.18 'Come into my parlour said the spider to the fly.' Explain what these two animals have:

(a) in common

(b) as differences between them. (2)

1.19 Make a table with two headings, *invertebrate* and *vertebrate*. Put the subheadings *backbone*, *no backbone* and the following animals into the correct part of your table:

octopus   cat   shark   spider   frog   crab   beetle   fox   (8)

1.20 A lizard is a reptile, while a newt is an amphibian. In many ways they look similar, yet they belong to different classes. Give reasons for this. (2)

1.4 Living things in their environment and in their habitats

Learn these terms:

- *Habitat*: the place where a living organism lives.
- *Environment*: factors affecting an organism, including:
  - biological factors (other plants and animals)
  - chemical factors (soil, minerals, fresh/salt water)
  - physical factors (water, wind, light, temperature).

Man-made changes that are harmful to the environment

- Loss of agricultural land (buildings, industry, mining, transport).
- Large-scale reduction of tropical rainforests.
- Reduction of fish stocks (more efficient catching, and pollution of waters; limiting growth of fish population).
- Pollution of the air due to burning of **fossil fuels**, e.g. acid rain, increase of carbon dioxide in the air.

Conservation – man-made ways of helping the environment

- National parks, wildlife centres, zoos.
- Protection of 'endangered species' and their habitats.
- Motor engines that are more efficient, to reduce harmful emissions produced when burning fossil fuels.
- Greater use of 'alternative' forms of energy (wind, geothermal) to reduce pollution from burning fossil fuels.
- Recycling of household waste to reduce landfill.

Adaptation – features of organisms that allow them to survive in their environment

- Protection: hard shells, prickles, ability to move quickly away from **predators**, camouflage (able to hide by blending in with surroundings).
- Hunting and feeding: sharp teeth, beaks, claws; big eyes, ears; able to move quickly.
- Light and length of day:
  - Spring: days become longer, triggering animal breeding, plant growth and seed germination.
  - Autumn: days become shorter triggering some animals to migrate to warmer places and others to hibernate ('sleep' during the winter).

  Some animals are active at night (e.g. badger, bat and hedgehog) and rest during the day and are said to be **nocturnal**.

- Temperature: fur, fatty layers of insulation in polar regions.
- Seasonal change:
  - Warming spring: increase in plant growth, return from **migration**; reproduction and growth during coming summer.
  - Cooling autumn: leaf fall from deciduous plants; preparation for migration/**hibernation**.

Feeding relationships (food chains)

A → B means A *is eaten by* B. The arrow points the way that energy moves up through the food chain. For example:

Rose leaves → Aphid → Ladybird → Robin

producer → **consumer** → **consumer** → **consumer**

Always a plant → Herbivore → Carnivore → Top carnivore in this chain

- Plants use sunlight energy to make food so are called producers.
- Organisms that eat other organisms are called consumers.
- Animals that eat only plants are called herbivores.
- Animals (predators) that eat other animals (**prey**) are called **carnivores**.
- Animals that eat plants and animals are called omnivores.

Remember, all food chains start with a plant.

? **Exam-style questions**

Try these questions. The answers are given at the back of the book.

1.21 List three ways in which man's activities have made changes to our natural environment. (3)

1.22 List three ways in which conservation of the environment can be carried out. (3)

1.23 (a) Name two fossil fuels. (2)

(b) Explain why the use of fossil fuels is causing problems for wildlife. (2)

1.24 Four food chains are given below:

A lettuce → rabbit → fox → flea

B oak tree → aphid → ladybird → robin

C grass → earthworm → shrew → owl

D algae → pond snail → leech → dragonfly nymph

(a) Which food chain occurs in water? (1)

(b) Which food chain does not contain a vertebrate? (1)

(c) In which food chain is the herbivore a mammal? (1)

(d) Which food chain does not contain an insect? (1)

(e) In which food chain is the producer very much larger than the herbivore? (1)

Looking at cells – using the light microscope

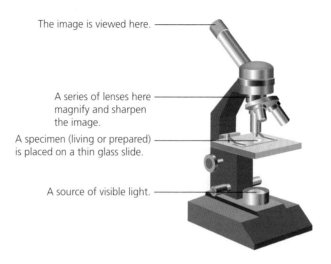

The image is viewed here.

A series of lenses here magnify and sharpen the image.

A specimen (living or prepared) is placed on a thin glass slide.

A source of visible light.

- The lens you look through is called the eyepiece.

- The lens nearest the object is the objective lens – there are usually at least two of these: low power, which magnifies 4 times and high power, which magnifies 40 times.

- Make sure the objective lens is set to low power at first.

- Provide a stream of light travelling up through the microscope.

- Place a slide on the stage. Secure with the stage clips.

- *Looking from the side*, turn the coarse focusing knob away from you to *wind down* the tube until the objective lens is as close to the specimen as possible – but *not* touching the slide.

- Looking through the eyepiece, turn the focus knob towards you, winding the tube upwards until the specimen comes clearly into view.

- Use the fine focus knob if fitted, to obtain a really clear picture.

- If high power is required, rotate the objective lens disc to the required position. Some fine focusing may be required.

Preparation of slides for the light microscope

- When mounting specimens, it is usual to put the specimen on the slide with a drop, or two, of mounting fluid – usually water.

- A cover slip is normally placed on top to provide a flat surface to help with focusing the microscope.

- Stains are sometimes used to enable us to see certain featues of a cell more clearly. There are many of these, but you may well have used two:

  - **Iodine**: often used for looking at plant cells.

    Nucleus will appear orange/yellow; starch grains will appear blue/black.

  - **Methylene blue**: often used for looking at animal cells.

    Nucleus will appear blue.

Specialised cells for specific jobs

Most larger organisms are multicellular, i.e. made up from a large number of cells of different types. Examples of cell types and their functions are given in the following table.

Type of cell	Shape	Function
Sperm cell	Contains male genes, long tail for swimming, large head	Fertilises female egg
Egg cell (ovum)	Larger than sperm, contains female genes	To divide cells and develop embryo after fertilisation
Muscle cell	Long, contains contractible fibrils	Becomes shorter to cause movement
Nerve cell	Long and thin	Carries messages round the body
Ciliated epithelial cells	Lining layer with little hairs (cilia)	Cilia trap dust and move it out of lungs
Root hair cells	Rectangular with 'hair' extension	'Hair' extends into soil to collect water and minerals

Tissues and organs

Specialised cells, generally of the same type, will combine together to make tissues, e.g. muscles or skin.

Sometimes tissues of various kinds combine to form an organ, which is a structure that performs a specific function.

● The leaf is an organ that is made from various types of plant tissue.

● The eye is an organ that is made from various types of animal tissue.

Each organ has a specific job to do and in more complex animals such as mammals, organs will combine into a system.

Separate systems do not work independently but work together to ensure the successful development and operation of the body.

Main systems in the human body

Name of system	What it does	Main organs in the system	Location of organs
Locomotion system	Supports the body and allows movement	Muscles and skeleton of bones	Throughout the body
Transport system	Takes food to all parts of body and removes waste from them	Heart and blood vessels	Throughout the body
Breathing system	Provides oxygen and removes carbon dioxide from body	Windpipe and lungs	Thorax
Nervous system (including sensory system)	Takes messages to/from all parts of the body via the brain	Brain, spinal cord, nerves, eyes, ears, nose, tongue	Brain – head; spinal cord – backbone; nerves – throughout the body
Digestive system	Breaks down food and absorbs useful chemicals into the blood	Gut, stomach, intestine, liver	Mouth – head; otherwise, mainly in the abdomen
Reproductive system	Produces/receives gametes for next generation	Testes, ovaries, uterus	Abdomen
Excretory system	Removes waste products	Kidneys, bladder, liver	Abdomen

Not examined
The nervous and excretory systems will not be examined in CE.

Structural adaptations of unicellular organisms

Most unicellular organisms live in water – they rely on soluble substances to pass in and out (diffusion) of the cell. Some have special structures that enable them to (i) exchange gases, (ii) feed and (iii) move.

Exchange gases

Cell membrane: this usually has a large surface area to allow oxygen in and carbon dioxide out and is a feature common to most unicellular organisms.

Feed

In amoeba, the membrane surrounds smaller organisms to form a food vacuole, which is able to digest and pass nutrients into the cytoplasm.

In *Euglena*, there are two methods of feeding:

● small food particles captured in a structure called the gullet

● photosynthesis as there are chloroplasts within the cytoplasm.

Move

In amoeba, the cytoplasm changes shape and flows, causing the animal to move forward.

In *Euglena*, a flagellum acts like an oar and swishes to and fro, moving the cell through the water.

? **Exam-style questions**

Try these questions. The answers are given at the back of the book.

2.1 Do all plant cells contain chloroplasts? Give a reason for your answer. (2)

2.2 (a) Draw a sperm cell and an egg cell. (2)

　　(b) Explain the differences in the shape/size of these cells. (2)

　　(c) What is the function of these cells? (2)

2.3 This question is about the human body. Draw the table below and complete it. (10)

Name of system	What it does	Main organs in the system
Locomotion		
Transport		
Respiratory		
Digestive		
Reproductive		

2.2 Nutrition and digestion

An intake of food provides:

- a supply of energy: required for all living activities
- materials that enable an organism to (i) grow, (ii) replace worn or damaged parts.

In general, food taken in by organisms consists of two parts:

- useful materials
- waste.

Food is broken down by digestion.

- Useful materials are absorbed into the cells.
- Waste materials are collected together as faeces and removed from the body by **egestion**.

Useful materials

Protein

- Used for growth and repair of cells.
- Found in meats, fish, milk, cheese, eggs, nuts, green vegetables and flour.

Carbohydrates

- **Compounds** containing the **elements** carbon, hydrogen and oxygen.
- Two main groups:
  - Sugars, e.g. **glucose** – these may be found in fruits, jams, soft drinks and sweets.
  - Starches (built up from sugars and stored in the muscles and liver until needed to be broken down into glucose for respiration) – these can be found in potatoes, nuts, rice, cereals, peas, beans, bread and cakes.

How to test for the presence of starch:

1. Crush solid foods into small pieces.
2. Add a few drops of iodine solution.
3. A colour change from brown to blue-black shows that **starch** is present.

How to test for the presence of sugar:

1. Crush food and add water to dissolve it.
2. Add Benedict's solution (add an equal volume).
3. Warm the mixture using a water bath (no open flame).
4. Sugar is present if a red/orange colour appears.

Lipids (fats and oils)

- Used as a store of energy (can be broken down into glucose for respiration) and also as a layer of insulation.
- Found in meats, dairy products and food fried in animal fats, e.g. chips.

Vitamins and minerals

- These are needed in small amounts to enable important chemical reactions to happen.

- They are not produced by the body, so have to be taken in with food.

Name	What it is needed for	Where found	Result of lack of it
Vitamin C	Tissue repair, resistance to disease	Fresh fruit and vegetables	Scurvy (bleeding gums), poor growth in children, tissue repair is very slow
Calcium	Making of bones, teeth and blood clotting	Dairy products, flour products, green vegetables	Poor bone development
Iron	Manufacture of red blood cells	Meat, green vegetables	Shortages of red blood cells

Water

- Present in every living cell and forms about 70% of our bodies.

- The blood system moves materials that have been dissolved in water.

- Egg and sperm cells move around our bodies in fluids that are mainly water.

- Humans lose about 1.5 litres of water each day in urine, sweat and breath.

- Water can be replaced as a drink or as foods, such as salads.

Fibre

- Comes from plants and is mainly indigestible.

- Provides bulk to enable food to travel through the digestive system more efficiently.

- Found in cereals, whole-grain bread and vegetables.

Balanced diet

All of the groups of nutrients listed above are needed.

- An all-meat diet provides a good source of **protein**, but also too much fat and almost no carbohydrate.

- An all-potato diet provides plenty of carbohydrate, but very little protein.

We need to have a mixture of foods to provide us with these in the right proportions. This is called a balanced diet.

Digestion

> **Not examined**
> Only basic digestion studied at 11+ is examined at CE, but extra information is included here for biological completeness.

Much of the food that we eat will consist of a mixture of proteins, **fats** and **carbohydrates**, which need to be broken down into smaller soluble molecules. Much of this breaking down will be carried out by enzymes. An important enzyme is amylase, which breaks starch into simple sugars.

Enzymes

- These are chemicals that enable other chemical reactions to happen.
- There is a different enzyme for each chemical reaction in the body.
- Enzymes do not change as they work, so can be used again.

Stages of digestion

Ingestion: food is taken into the mouth.

↓

Physical digestion: teeth cut and break down food, which is mixed with saliva produced in the mouth.

↓

Chemical digestion: action of enzymes and stomach acids breaks down food into small, soluble molecules, which can be dissolved in the blood.

↓

Absorption: soluble food molecules move across the villi, which are part of the walls of the small intestine, into the bloodstream, which carries them to the liver for sorting, then to all parts of the body.

↓

Assimilation: digested food is used by the cells for growth and repair.

↓

Egestion: in the large intestine, undigested food mixed with fibre becomes faeces and passes out through the anus.

? Exam-style questions

Try these questions. The answers are given at the back of the book.

2.4 Below is a table showing relative amounts of different nutrients in food that might be eaten at breakfast.

Food	Carbohydrate (g per 100 g)	Fat (g per 100 g)	Protein (g per 100 g)
Orange juice	8	0	0
Bacon	0	10	12
Egg	0	5	6
Bread	24	Very small	4
Butter	0	8	Very small

(a) Select a food that is a good supply of energy. (1)

(b) Select two foods that are good for bodybuilding and growth. (2)

(c) What is the main carbohydrate found in:

    (i) orange juice

    (ii) bread? (2)

(d) Name two important nutrients not included in the table. (2)

2.5 The following table shows the average daily amounts of protein that human males, of different ages, require if they are to remain fit and healthy.

Age (in years)	11	14	18	25	45	65
Protein requirement (in g per day)	75	85	100	65	65	65

Explain the differences in protein requirement for human males at ages 18 and 45. (4)

	Snack X	Snack Y
Fat	22%	34%
Fibre	18%	35%
Carbohydrate	60%	31%

(a) (i) Which snack contains the greatest amount of fibre? (1)

(ii) Suggest why fibre is an important part of your diet. (1)

(b) (i) Which snack would you eat before running a race? (1)

(ii) Give a reason for your answer. (1)

2.7 Vitamins and minerals are important parts of our diets. Give one example of each, suggesting what they do. (4)

2.3 Gas exchange systems including cellular respiration

Breathing in humans

- The main organs for gas exchange are the lungs, which are located in the thorax (chest).

- The thorax is lined with a membrane and the floor of the thorax is separated from the abdomen by a flexible membrane called the diaphragm.

- Muscular action by the intercostal muscles located between the ribs causes the diaphragm to move up and down, allowing air to move in and out of the lungs during breathing.

- Air moves in and out through the nose and throat, which is connected to the windpipe (trachea).

- In the lungs, the trachea branches into two smaller tubes, one branch (bronchus) supplying each lung.

- Each bronchus divides into smaller branches (bronchioles), which divide again and again.

- At the end of each of the tiniest branches are little air sacs, which are surrounded by blood vessels.

Note: It is not true to say we breathe in oxygen and breathe out carbon dioxide. We breathe in air, most of which is nitrogen.

	Approximate content of inhaled air	Approximate content of exhaled air
Nitrogen	78%	80%
Oxygen	20%	16%
Carbon dioxide	0.04%	4%

Two important lung volumes are:

- tidal volume – the amount of air breathed in or out normally (measured in dm^3)

- vital capacity – the maximum amount breathed with the deepest breath.

Lung capacity is increased by regular outdoor exercise.

Asthma

Asthma is a medical condition that causes muscles in the airways to contract, making it difficult to breathe. This is caused by a variety of factors, including anxiety, pollen, household dust and air pollution. Use of an inhaler that blows a spray of chemicals to relax the airway muscles is one method of providing relief.

Dangers of smoking tobacco

Tobacco smoke contains substances that harm the lungs, heart and circulation. The smoke is acidic and contains many chemicals that damage human tissue. Three of the most damaging are listed below:

- Nicotine: damages blood vessels leading to increase of blood pressure and risk of heart disease; causes addiction.
- Tar: causes lung cancer; blocks the action of cilia, which sweep away dust and microbes.
- Carbon monoxide: reduces supply of oxygen to the cells; contributes to disease of the heart and arteries.

Smoking tobacco is strongly advised against for asthma sufferers.

Respiration

Respiration is *not* breathing. Respiration is a series of chemical reactions carried out within each living cell to release energy for all life processes.

There are two types of respiration: aerobic and anaerobic.

Aerobic respiration

Aerobic respiration can be summarised by the following equation:

glucose + oxygen $\rightarrow$ carbon dioxide + water + energy

- Glucose comes from digested foods.
- Oxygen comes from the air inhaled into the lungs during breathing. So this form of respiration is called aerobic (aer = air) respiration.
- Glucose and oxygen are called reactants.
- Carbon dioxide and water are waste products.
- Both reactants and products are carried to and from the cells in the bloodstream (also called the circulatory system).
- Oxygen enters and carbon dioxide leaves the bloodstream by passing through the walls of air sacs, which are part of the lungs. This is known as gas exchange.

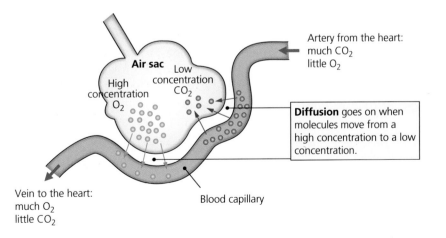

Artery from the heart: much CO_2 little O_2

Air sac Low concentration CO_2

High concentration O_2

Diffusion goes on when molecules move from a high concentration to a low concentration.

Vein to the heart: much O_2 little CO_2

Blood capillary

Anaerobic respiration

Anaerobic respiration (no oxygen involved) can be summarised by the following equations.

In animals:

glucose → carbon dioxide + lactic acid + little energy (15× less than
aerobic respiration)

In plants and yeast:

glucose → carbon dioxide + ethanol + little energy

This reaction is called fermentation and is at the heart of the alcoholic drinks and baking industries.

The holes in bread are caused by the production of carbon dioxide during the anaerobic respiration of the yeast – the bread is said to have risen. Any ethanol produced is removed during the baking.

> **? Exam-style questions**
>
> Try these questions. The answers are given at the back of the book.
>
> 2.8 (a) What does the word *respiration* describe? (2)
>
> (b) Where, in an organism, does respiration take place? (1)
>
> 2.9 (a) Write down the word equation that represents aerobic respiration. (6)
>
> (b) What does the term *aerobic* mean? (1)
>
> 2.10 (a) In which part of the lungs does gas exchange take place? (1)
>
> (b) During this process, state what happens to (i) oxygen;
> (ii) carbon dioxide. (1)
>
> 2.11 It is often said that, 'We breathe in oxygen and breathe out carbon dioxide'. Explain why this statement is not completely correct. (2)
>
> 2.12 List three substances that enter the body because of smoking and say in which way each substance is harmful to the body. (6)

2.4 Health

Healthy lifestyle

Humans can choose whether their lifestyle is healthy or not.

A healthy lifestyle depends upon three main factors:

- A balanced diet: a mix of protein, carbohydrate, fats, fibre, water, minerals and vitamins is needed for growth and repair/replacement of cells. Overeating of fatty and sugary foods can lead to being overweight (obese), which puts an extra strain on the heart as more energy is required to carry out life processes, e.g. movement.

- Taking regular exercise: greater intake of air during exercise causes the muscles of the heart to beat faster and so remain healthy, resulting in less chance of heart disease. Excess fat in the body is reduced by exercise.

- Avoiding intake of harmful substances:

  - Smoking leads to lung, circulatory system and heart problems.

  - Alcohol slows reactions and excess amounts cause damage to the liver, stomach and heart.

  - Drugs (other than those prescribed for medical reasons) introduce chemicals into our bodies that upset the finely balanced chemical mechanisms that exist to keep all our life functions working properly. Solvents, aerosols, LSD, ecstasy are examples of substances that badly damage the brain and heart.

Fighting disease

Diseases are either non-infectious (not caught from somebody else) or infectious (caught from somebody else).

Causes of infectious diseases

Minute microorganisms (microbes) divide and reproduce very rapidly and can damage cells or release toxins (poisons) that can make you feel very ill.

Viruses:

- Must invade a living cell to reproduce, eventually causing damage to the cell.

- When they are in a host cell, viruses cannot be destroyed without damaging the cell.

- Viruses cannot be controlled by antibiotics.

- Examples of diseases caused by viruses include influenza ('flu), common cold, AIDS.

Bacteria:

- Live and grow outside living cells.

- Can reproduce every 20 minutes.

- Are bigger than viruses, but smaller than cells.

- Can be killed by: antibiotics – taken as medicine; antiseptics – on the skin; disinfectants – on kitchen and bathroom surfaces.

- Examples of diseases caused by bacteria include cholera, tetanus, food poisoning.

Natural defences

Our body has three natural defences against disease: barriers, white blood cells and blood clots.

- Skin, wax in ears, tears in eyes all form barriers to keep microbes away from the body's tissues.

- Open wounds are protected from microbes by blood clots, which are produced by a special type of blood cell (platelet), forming a scab.

Human actions

Personal hygiene:

- Regular washing of hands, hair and the body removes bacteria, which cause body odours, infestations in hair and spread of food poisoning.
- Regular brushing of teeth removes bacteria that cause tooth decay.

Community actions:

- Provision of safe, clean drinking water.
- Removal and safe disposal of refuse and sewage.
- Provision of medical care.

Provision of medical care:

- Immunisation.
- Medicines such as antibiotics.

? Exam-style questions

Try these questions. The answers are given at the back of the book.

2.13 (a) What does the term *obese* mean? (2)

(b) How does a human become obese? (2)

(c) What problems are caused by a person being obese? (2)

2.14 If a bacterium could divide into two every 20 minutes, how many bacteria would there be after 3 hours? (2)

2.5 Reproduction in animals and plants

Reproduction in humans

- Sexual reproduction requires two individuals (parents), male and female.
- During adolescence humans develop reproductive organs, which produce the sex cells – **sperm** (male) and **ova** (female) – called **gametes**.
- The gametes are brought together (during copulation) and fuse to form a fertilised egg (**zygote**).
- The zygote will, after much cell division, grow into an embryo, which then develops into a new individual.

Adolescence – a time of physical change

- Occurs between the ages of 10 and 20.
- Body hair starts growing, e.g. hair around the genitals (pubic hair).
- In males, hair grows on the chest and face and the voice becomes deeper.
- In females, the menstrual cycle begins.
- Reproductive organs develop, e.g. in males, penis becomes larger; in females, breasts develop and hips become wider.

Adolescence – a time of emotional change

- Boys and girls become more independent and more responsible for their thoughts and actions.

- Boys and girls become more aware of the opposite sex.

- As there is great variation in the time when the changes begin and also in the nature and size of these, some people may become anxious because they appear to develop earlier or later than their friends.

The menstrual cycle

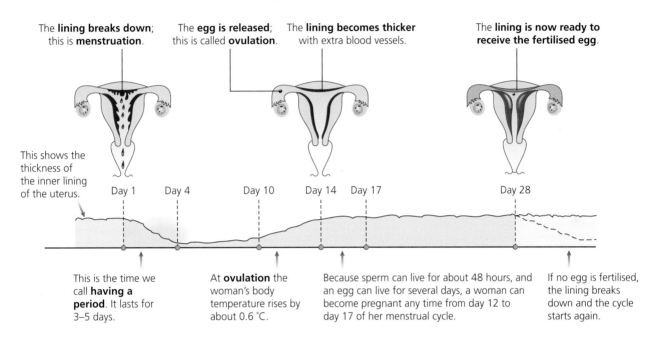

The **lining breaks down**; this is **menstruation**.

The **egg is released**; this is called **ovulation**.

The **lining becomes thicker** with extra blood vessels.

The **lining is now ready to receive the fertilised egg**.

This shows the thickness of the inner lining of the uterus.

Day 1   Day 4   Day 10   Day 14   Day 17   Day 28

This is the time we call **having a period**. It lasts for 3–5 days.

At **ovulation** the woman's body temperature rises by about 0.6 °C.

Because sperm can live for about 48 hours, and an egg can live for several days, a woman can become pregnant any time from day 12 to day 17 of her menstrual cycle.

If no egg is fertilised, the lining breaks down and the cycle starts again.

Fertilisation and implantation

- During sexual intercourse, special sponge tissue (erectile tissue) within the penis becomes full of blood, which enables the penis to become stiff enough to enter the female's vagina.

- Movement of the penis within the vagina causes a nervous reflex that is a signal for over 300 million sperms contained in about 4–5 cm³ of fluid to be ejaculated out of the penis into the vagina.

- One egg is released by the female every 28 days and is carried by cilia into the oviduct.

- Only a small proportion of sperms will complete the journey to the oviduct and it is here that only one sperm will fuse with the egg to form a **zygote**.

- The zygote contains genes from both the mother and father.

- The zygote begins cell division until a ball of about 128 cells (now called an embryo) arrives in the uterus and settles deep in the newly formed thick lining.

- This settling process is called **implantation**.

- Once the embryo is implanted, the mother is said to be **pregnant**.

Development of the embryo

- The implanted embryo develops into the **fetus** by means of cell division and specialisation.
- The fetus is contained within a sac (amniotic sac filled with amniotic fluid) and is attached to the placenta by the umbilical cord. The amniotic fluid keeps the fetus moist and protects it against physical knocks.

The placenta

- The placenta is a plate-shaped organ that grows deep into the uterus wall and increases in size as the fetus develops.
- It enables food and oxygen to be passed to the fetus and carbon dioxide together with waste materials to be removed from the fetus.
- Although the mother's blood system flows close to the blood vessels of the fetus, the two are entirely different systems.
- The blood of the mother and the blood of the fetus do not mix. This is because:
  - The blood group of the fetus may be different from that of the mother. Bloods of different groups must not be mixed together.
  - The mother's blood pressure will be much higher than that of the fetus.

The umbilical cord

- The cord contains blood vessels that:
  - take oxygen and food to the fetus
  - take carbon dioxide and nitrogenous waste away from the fetus.
- It is clamped at birth to prevent bleeding and then cut. The 'belly button' is the remains of the umbilical cord.

Care during pregnancy

Pregnant mothers should be careful about their lifestyle and diet. This is because:

- smoking and alcohol intake by the mother, together with germs from diseases, could result in harmful materials being passed to the fetus through the umbilical cord
- excess physical activity may harm the fetus.

Birth

- After a gestation period of about 40 weeks (9 months), labour begins with contractions of the uterus.
- Contractions cause the amniotic sac to burst and fluid flows out of the vagina; this is called the breaking of the waters.
- Further contractions push the baby, head first, out into the world.
- After birth, the umbilical cord is clamped and then cut.

Reproduction in flowering plants

The variety of plants depends upon the process of sexual reproduction, which is the fusion of male and female sex cells that are made in the sex organs. The process of carrying male pollen to a female stigma is called **pollination**. The fusion of a male pollen with a female **ovule** is called **fertilisation**.

1   Male sex organ: **stamen** (**anther** + **filament**).

     Female sex organ: **carpel** (**stigma** + **style** + **ovary**).

2   Male sex cells: pollen – made in the anther.

     Female sex cells: ovules – made in the ovary.

3   Pollination: the transfer of pollen from anther to stigma by various ways:

     • Anther and stigma in same flower (self-pollination); anther and stigma in different flowers of the same type or species (cross-pollination).

     • Pollen carried from anther to stigma by (a) insect, or (b) wind.

4   Fertilisation: the fusing of the sex cell pollen and ovule:

     • Pollen grain grows a tube when it lands on the stigma.

     • Pollen tube grows down through the style and enters the ovule through a small hole.

     • Male sex cell travels down the pollen tube and fuses with the female sex cell in the ovule.

5   Fertilised ovule develops into a seed.

6   Wall of ovary changes and becomes a fruit. It contains and protects the seed(s).

7   Seeds are dispersed so that new plants do not compete with parent plant for nutrients, light, water and space. Seeds can be dispersed in various ways; for example:

     • Animals tempted by the fleshy fruit, which contains indigestible seeds.

     • Wind carries seeds with parachutes (dandelion) or wings (sycamore) away from parent plant.

8   The dormant seed awakens or germinates into a new plant.

 Revision tip

WOW!

   Water

        Oxygen

             Warmth

All are needed for a seed to be able to germinate.

Photosynthesis releases oxygen into the air

- Before the arrival of green plants on the Earth, there was no oxygen at all in the atmosphere.

- Photosynthesis produces more oxygen than the plant needs for respiration, so excess oxygen is released into the atmosphere through the stomata (little holes on the underside of leaves).

- As a result of the evolution and development of green plants, the amount of oxygen in the atmosphere has built up to its present level of about 20% of all the gases in the air. So every leaf and blade of grass helps to maintain the amount of oxygen in the air.

- Oxygen needs to be replaced because respiration by all organisms (including plants) removes vast quantities of oxygen from the air every minute. If this oxygen were not replaced by photosynthesis, then all the oxygen would be removed from the air in a few thousand years.

Photosynthesis recycles carbon

The element carbon is present in *all* living organisms and fossil fuels.

Organism	Carbon content
Animals	About 20%
Plants	About 40%
Fossil fuels (coal)	About 90%

- Carbon atoms can join with each other to form chains or rings to produce the complex organic compounds that are found in all living organisms.

- Hydrocarbons contain carbon and hydrogen (e.g. natural gas, crude oil – a mixture of many hydrocarbons).

- Carbohydrates contain carbon, hydrogen and oxygen (e.g. sugars, starches).

- Photosynthesis uses carbon dioxide and water to produce carbohydrates (biomass).

- Photosynthesis increases biomass and reduces the amount of carbon dioxide in the air.

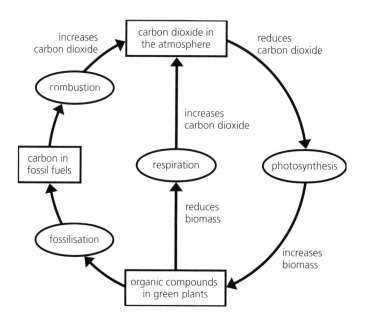

- Respiration uses oxygen to change carbohydrate (biomass) into carbon dioxide and water, with energy being released.
- Respiration reduces biomass and increases the amount of carbon dioxide in the air.

Human actions affecting the balance of gases in the air

- Burning fossil fuels *increases* the amount of carbon dioxide in the air.
- Cutting down forests *reduces* the amount of photosynthesis, so the amount of carbon dioxide in the air increases because less is being used up.

Photosynthesis – the process

1 Part played by chloroplasts

- Energy from the Sun is absorbed within the **chloroplasts**, which contain the green pigment chlorophyll, which reacts with light.
- Chloroplasts are found in the cytoplasm of nearly every leaf and stem cell and it is these that give plants their green colour. Plants have a central stem. This carries specialised tubes such as the phloem, which transports sugar to the growing areas, and xylem, which transports water to the leaf. The central vein in a leaf branches into smaller veins that are able to reach the flat surfaces of the leaf. Most of the chlorophyll will be found in the upper layers of the leaf, which are closest to the light. On the underside of the leaf will be little holes (**stomata**) that are able to open and close to enable the gas exchanges detailed below to happen.
- There are *no* chloroplasts within root cells, as photosynthesis will not happen underground where there is no light.

2 Parts played by carbon dioxide and water

- These two substances provide the ingredients (carbon, hydrogen, oxygen), for the making of carbohydrates.
- **Water** is a supply of hydrogen; carbon dioxide supplies carbon and oxygen.

The series of reactions that make up the process of photosynthesis may be summarised by the following word equation:

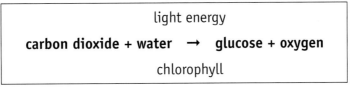

light energy

carbon dioxide + water → glucose + oxygen

chlorophyll

- Carbon dioxide and water are the reactants – glucose (a carbohydrate) and oxygen are the products of photosynthesis.

What happens to the products of photosynthesis?

Oxygen:

- Some of this will be used by the plant itself, for respiration.
- Oxygen not used by the plant will be released through the stomata – see above.

Glucose for respiration:

- Photosynthesis provides the glucose, which is needed by every living cell, for respiration.
- The leaves make more glucose than they need, so glucose is transported to other parts of the plant for respiration.

Glucose for making living material – increasing biomass:

● For growth, plants need a constant supply of proteins and fats, which can be made from sugars such as glucose.

● To make proteins, nitrogen will be needed as well as sugars.

● To make chlorophyll, magnesium will be needed as well as sugars.

Changing glucose into starch:

● In good light (daytime), glucose is made at a faster rate than the rate at which it can be transported away, so this excess glucose is changed into starch.

● In darkness (night), starch in the leaves is changed back into glucose and transported to other parts of the plant.

● Food, in the form of starch, is stored in preparation for the growth of the next generation:

  • in seeds (peas and beans)

  • in storage organs such as bulbs (onions) and tubers (potatoes)

  • in specialised root systems (carrots, parsnips).

Testing that light is needed for photosynthesis to take place and for presence of starch

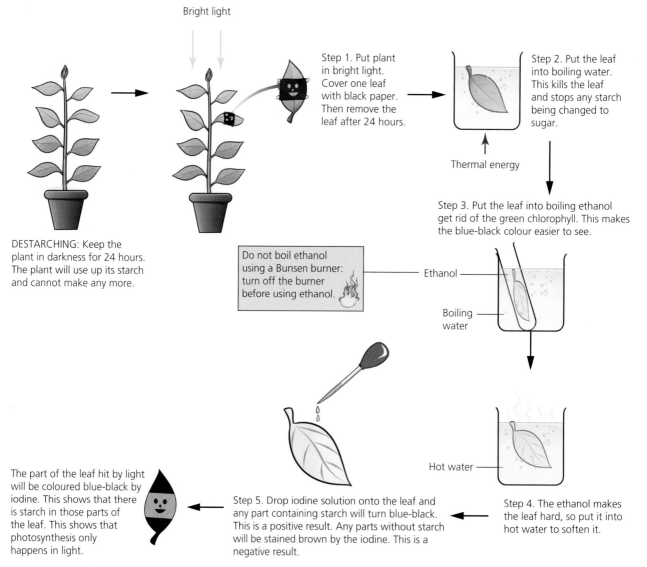

Bright light

Step 1. Put plant in bright light. Cover one leaf with black paper. Then remove the leaf after 24 hours.

Step 2. Put the leaf into boiling water. This kills the leaf and stops any starch being changed to sugar.

Thermal energy

Step 3. Put the leaf into boiling ethanol get rid of the green chlorophyll. This makes the blue-black colour easier to see.

Do not boil ethanol using a Bunsen burner: turn off the burner before using ethanol.

Ethanol

Boiling water

DESTARCHING: Keep the plant in darkness for 24 hours. The plant will use up its starch and cannot make any more.

Hot water

The part of the leaf hit by light will be coloured blue-black by iodine. This shows that there is starch in those parts of the leaf. This shows that photosynthesis only happens in light.

Step 5. Drop iodine solution onto the leaf and any part containing starch will turn blue-black. This is a positive result. Any parts without starch will be stained brown by the iodine. This is a negative result.

Step 4. The ethanol makes the leaf hard, so put it into hot water to soften it.

Testing that photosynthesis produces oxygen as a waste gas

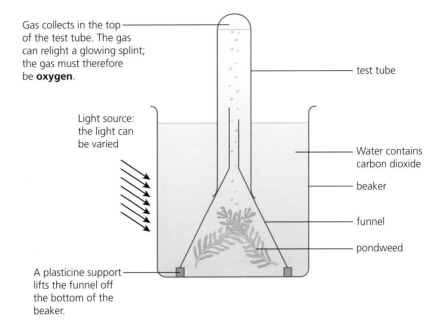

Gas collects in the top of the test tube. The gas can relight a glowing splint; the gas must therefore be **oxygen**.

Light source: the light can be varied

A plasticine support lifts the funnel off the bottom of the beaker.

test tube

Water contains carbon dioxide

beaker

funnel

pondweed

Requirements for growth and healthy plants

Water

- Plants will absorb water from the surrounding soil through the root system.
- Water enters the root system through very thin-walled specialised cells called root hairs.

How does a plant *use* the water it obtains through the roots?

- As a raw material for photosynthesis.
- As a solvent for sugars and starches, to enable them to be moved around the plant easily.
- As a solvent for minerals, to enable them to be transported to the place where they will be made into the proteins and chemicals that are essential to the growth and development of the plant.
- To maintain physical strength of the plant by keeping the cells turgid. (Within each cell, the central vacuole is full of sap, which has a high water content that presses outwards, making the cell rigid – or turgid).

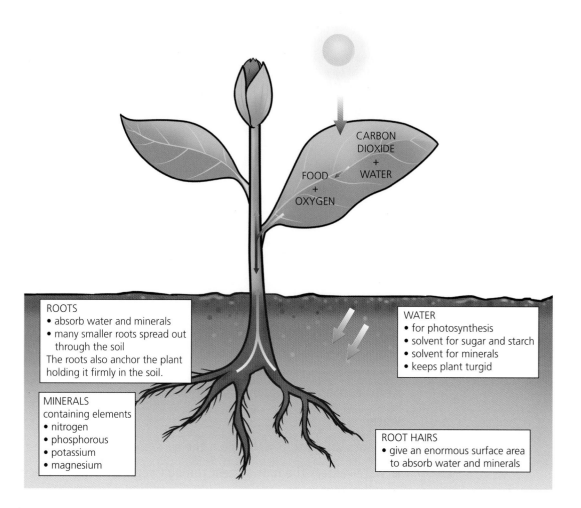

ROOTS
• absorb water and minerals
• many smaller roots spread out through the soil
The roots also anchor the plant holding it firmly in the soil.

MINERALS
containing elements
• nitrogen
• phosphorous
• potassium
• magnesium

WATER
• for photosynthesis
• solvent for sugar and starch
• solvent for minerals
• keeps plant turgid

ROOT HAIRS
• give an enormous surface area to absorb water and minerals

CARBON DIOXIDE + WATER

FOOD + OXYGEN

Mineral salts

Apart from oxygen, water and carbon dioxide, a healthy plant needs supplies of the following elements:

- Nitrogen (as nitrates) – to make proteins that are present in all parts of the plant.

- Magnesium – for production of chlorophyll inside the chloroplasts.

  • All these elements will be obtained from the soil surrounding the plant in the form of **mineral salts** that are soluble in water, e.g. nitrogen in the form of nitrates.

  • Soluble mineral salts will enter the plant through the thin-walled cells called root hair cells.

  • The large number of root hair cells increases the surface area of the root in contact with the soil, which enables water and soluble minerals to enter the plant more easily.

2.7 Variation, classification and inheritance

Variation

Although humans belong to the same species of animal (*Homo sapiens*), there are clearly differences between individuals called variations.

- Colour of eyes, blood group, face shape and whether you are male or female are variations between humans that result only from genes that are inherited from parents. These variations are called discontinuous variations.

- Discontinuous variations enable easy sorting of organisms; there are no in-between groups, e.g. one is either male or female.

- Height, shape, weight and build are variations that result both from inherited genes and the environment. Clearly, the amount of food intake and exercise will have an effect on all of these variations as well as those caused by the passing on of genes. These variations are called continuous variations.

- Continuous variations are not easy to put into discrete groups as there are many groups for each particular feature, e.g. size of chest.

Classification

- The variations described above occur within species of organisms. Variations between species can be used to sort organisms into groups.

- Sorting organisms into groups is called **classification**.

- The largest groups of organisms are known as **kingdoms**.

- The smallest groups are known as **species**. Differences between species can be identified by producing and using keys (see Chapter 1, 1.3 Variation and classification).

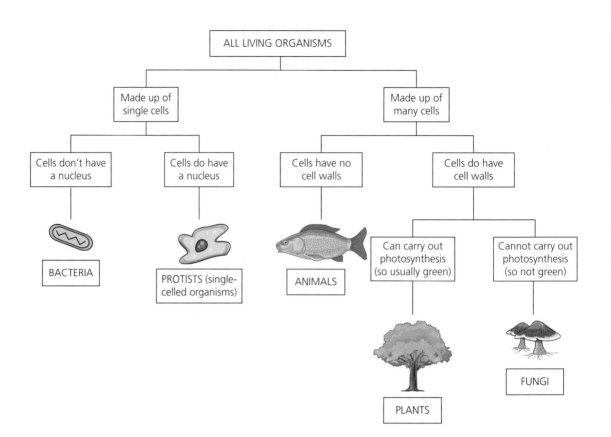

Why are fungi and green plants in different kingdoms?

● Green plants have chloroplasts and make their own food by photosynthesis.

● Fungi feed on the dead remains of other organisms. They do not have any chloroplasts.

The animal kingdom

Invertebrates

Invertebrates have no backbone. Main groups within a kingdom are called **phyla** (sing. phylum).

Arthropoda is an important invertebrate phylum. All animals in this phylum have:

● jointed limbs in pairs (arthro = jointed; poda = limbs)

● a hard outer covering (exoskeleton) made of chitin or limestone

● bodies divided into segments (compartments).

This is the largest of all animal groups and is divided into four main classes:

● Insects – bee, fly, beetle

● Arachnids – spider, scorpion, mite, tick

● Crustaceans – prawn, lobster, crab, woodlouse (on land)

● Myriapods – centipede, millipede

The differences between insects and arachnids are outlined in the following table.

Insects	Arachnids
3 body parts: head; thorax; abdomen	2 body parts: head/thorax; abdomen
6 legs (3 pairs)	8 legs (4 pairs)
Antennae	No antennae
Usually 2 pairs of wings	No wings

Vertebrates

Vertebrates have a backbone made of interlocking bones called vertebrae. These protect the nerve cord, which is connected to the brain. The brain is located in the skull and so is itself protected by bone.

Vertebrates are members of a single phylum in which there are five main groups (classes) of vertebrate:

Class	Features	Examples
Fish	All live in water; bodies covered in scales; lay eggs in water; cold-blooded	Haddock, cod, shark
Amphibians	Live on land and/or water; moist, smooth skin; lay eggs in water; cold-blooded	Frog, toad, newt
Reptiles	Scaly skin; live on land and/or water; lay shelled eggs on land; cold-blooded	Snake, crocodile, turtle
Birds	Skin covered in feathers; lay shelled eggs on land; warm-blooded	Eagle, blackbird, emu
Mammals	Skin covered in hair or fur; young born alive and fed by milk produced in the mother's mammary glands; warm-blooded	Dog, elephant, whale, man

- Cold-blooded animals – body temperature changes according to the temperature of the surrounding air or water.

- Warm-blooded animals – keep a constant body temperature.

The plant kingdom

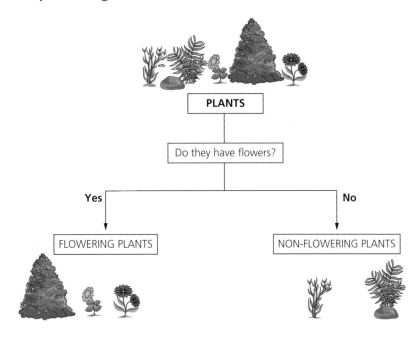

Inheritance

- Similarities between you and your father, mother and grandparents are direct evidence that each generation passes on features (**characteristics**) of themselves to future generations.

- Characteristics are determined by **genes**, which are found on the chromosomes in every cell nucleus. Each chromosome will contain a large number of genes, each one being responsible for passing on a particular characteristic.

- This passing of characteristics from one generation to another is known as **inheritance** and the study of inheritance is known as **genetics**.

- Inheritance is not a random process. In 1866 an Austrian monk, **Gregor Mendel**, conducted experiments with pea plants over a number of generations and was able to work out some basic laws of genetics.

> **?** Exam-style questions
>
> Try these questions. The answers are given at the back of the book.
>
> 2.25 Grass, rabbits and mushrooms are all organisms found in a wood, and yet they are all placed in different kingdoms. Explain why. (3)
>
> 2.26 To which type of variation do weight and athletic ability belong and from what do these result? (2)

2.8 Relationships in an ecosystem

Life, as we know it, without green plants would not exist at all.

- There would be no oxygen in the atmosphere.

- There would be no food – vegetables, salads, fruit or meat from animals that have fed on plants.

The *most important* resource on Earth is the fertile soil, which is necessary to grow plants.

- Rock and sand change into fertile soil by the addition of humus.

- **Humus** is plant and animal material that has been decayed by fungi and/or bacteria.

Life depends upon the interaction of a variety of living organisms. The study of this interaction is known as **ecology**.

Some key words

Habitat

All organisms need a place to live that will provide them with:

- food

- shelter

- protection from predators.

The place where a living organism lives is called its habitat. Examples of habitats include a pond, a field, a hedgerow, a wood, your house.

Community

- This refers to all of the living organisms within a habitat.

- The community will consist of a collection of populations.

- A population is a collection of organisms of the same species.

- A habitat (a place) and the communities (populations of living organisms), add together to make an ecosystem.

Ecology

This is the study of ecosystems – how communities interact with each other and their habitat.

An aquarium as an example of an ecosystem:

- Algae on the sides of the tank provide food for water snails.

- Water snails help to keep the water clear by eating algae.

- Water snails will need a supply of oxygen, so water plants will be needed to oxygenate the water as they carry out photosynthesis.

- If the growth of plants remains unchecked, they will eventually cover the surface of the water and so block out the light that is needed for photosynthesis.

- If there is no photosynthesis there will be no oxygen – water will become stale and unfit for animals.

- Clearly, the removal of the water would be a disaster for all animals and plants!

If the correct proportion of animals and plants is maintained, then the water conditions will be good enough to produce a balanced ecosystem – which will last and thrive.

Ecosystems that are not balanced soon disappear, providing immense problems for the communities that had existed in them. Protection of local habitats, together with protection of the Earth's natural resources will enable sustainable development of organisms.

The Earth's natural resources (oil, gas, coal, minerals) are finite. This means that there is only so much in the ground. Our use of these is increasing and we need to ensure that we use them carefully, for when they are all used up, they are gone forever. Difficult decisions lie ahead for humans as we all need homes and transport systems that eat into agricultural land that is required to feed an ever-increasing population.

Environment

This describes the conditions within an ecosystem. These conditions are known as environmental factors and are made up of two parts.

Physical factors (non-living factors) include:

- amount of water

- light

- temperature

- pH (acidity/alkalinity)

- wind.

Biological factors – the effect of other living organisms in the habitat – include:

- Predators/prey. Predators eat other animals (prey).
- Competitors. **Competition** arises when animals and plants compete for space, water, minerals and light.
  - Vegetable gardens are weeded to give crops maximum nutrients and space.
  - Animals will compete for 'territory' and a space to live.

Adaptation

This refers to the features of animals and plants that enable them to live successfully in their environment or respond to changes in their habitat.

Adaptation in plants:

- Grass has growing points very close to the ground, so when the lush green leaves are grazed by animals, or mowed by humans, the grass will grow again.
- Cacti have no leaves, in order to reduce water loss:
  - They are able to store water and have very deep roots for times of drought.
  - They have spines to prevent animals eating them.
- Pine needles are true leaves that are curled with the stomata on the inside to prevent water loss in the dry, windy conditions in which pine trees live.

Adaptation in animals:

- Polar bears and penguins have extra layers of fat to protect them from the sub-zero temperatures of the Arctic and Antarctic.
- Camels in the desert have feet with a large surface area so they do not sink into soft sand. They can store a lot of water and lose very little water in sweat. Their sandy colour gives them good camouflage from predators in the desert.

Population

This refers to the numbers of organisms of the same species, which exist in a habitat.

Populations will increase due to:

- birth of new individuals
- individuals moving in (**immigration**).

They will decrease due to:

- death of individuals
- individuals moving out (**emigration**).

Factors limiting population growth

- *Food shortage* – food supplies need to increase as populations increase in order to avoid intense competition for dwindling food supplies.
- *Shortage of space* – overcrowding leads to a quicker spread of disease, lack of living area and an increase in agitation and stress.

- *Predation* – predators moving in will reduce numbers of individuals, slowing population growth.

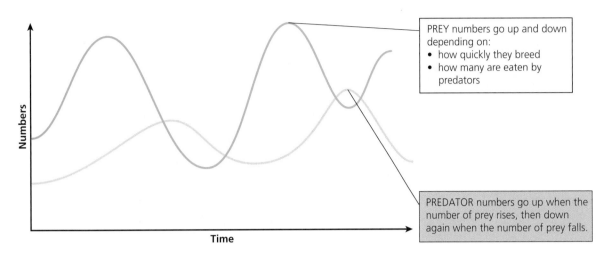

PREY numbers go up and down depending on:
- how quickly they breed
- how many are eaten by predators

PREDATOR numbers go up when the number of prey rises, then down again when the number of prey falls.

- *Increase in toxins (poisons)* – nitrogenous waste from animals will change into ammonia, which is a poison to most animals. Increase of populations will cause a build-up of toxins, which will limit population growth. Man's effect on the environment also increases toxins, for example:

  - by the use of insecticides

  - by lead and mercury poisoning the environment

  - by the increased use of fertilisers – particularly nitrates, which become washed into rivers and streams causing algae to grow at a rapid rate and resulting in unbalanced ecosystems.

Sampling and estimating the size of a population using a quadrat

- Place quadrat on the ground.
- Count numbers of organisms of a particular species inside the quadrat.
- Repeat this for a sample of several quadrats and calculate the mean – call this N.
- Count the total number of quadrats needed to study a particular area – call this Q.

total population = $N \times Q$

Food chains

Prey and predator form part of a **food chain** in which each organism provides the food for the next organism in the chain.

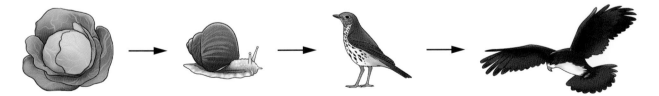

In this food chain:

- Lettuce is the primary producer. The primary producer is always a plant.
- Snail is the primary **consumer**. The primary consumer is always a herbivore.
- Thrush is a secondary consumer. The secondary consumer is always a carnivore or omnivore.
- Hawk is a tertiary consumer and is the top carnivore in this chain.

What do arrows in a food chain mean?

In simple terms, A → B means A is eaten by B.

- The arrow shows the direction in which energy is transferred in a food chain.
- Some energy is used for the living processes of each of the organisms.
- Energy is lost to the environment – usually as heat – at every stage of a food chain, so only about 10% passes from one stage to the next.

Food webs

A **food web** is a set of interconnected food chains. This means that consumers have more than one supply of food.

TOP CARNIVORES: Foxes and buzzards are at the top of this food web because nothing else eats them. There can only be very few top carnivores because each one of them needs to consume many organisms 'lower down' in the web.

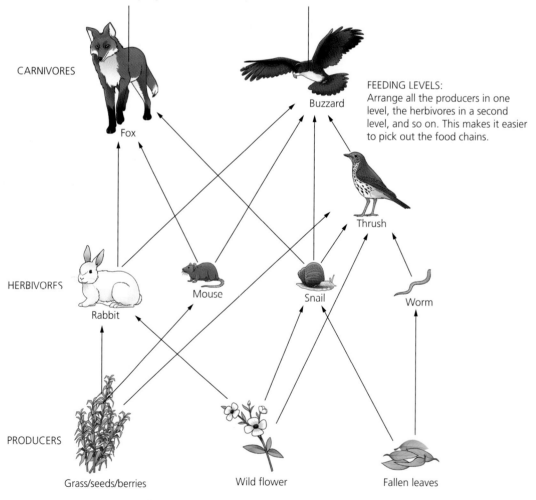

CARNIVORES

Fox

Buzzard

FEEDING LEVELS:
Arrange all the producers in one level, the herbivores in a second level, and so on. This makes it easier to pick out the food chains.

Thrush

HERBIVORFS

Rabbit

Mouse

Snail

Worm

PRODUCERS

Grass/seeds/berries

Wild flower

Fallen leaves

Decay is part of a food web:

- When a body dies, the dead body is broken down by bacteria and fungi.

- Decomposers break down dead remains into simple chemicals such as nitrates that enrich the soil.

- Enriched soil enables plants (primary producers) to grow, thrive and support the food web.

★ Make sure you know

★ The main components of a cell and different cells.

★ The main systems in the human body.

★ The various elements that make up our nutrition and what these are used for.

★ How humans move.

★ How humans reproduce.

★ What happens during respiration.

★ How humans breathe.

★ What is involved in leading a healthy lifestyle.

★ How we fight disease.

★ Photosynthesis and its part in increasing biomass.

★ That photosynthesis increases oxygen and decreases carbon dioxide in the air.

★ The process of photosynthesis, and how to test for presence of starch and oxygen.

★ What plants need to enable them to grow and be healthy.

★ The differences between organisms of the same species, which is called variation.

★ About continuous and discontinuous variation.

★ Classification as the way we sort organisms into groups, e.g. the five kingdoms.

★ The differences between insects and spiders.

★ Features of the five classes of vertebrate animals.

★ That ecology is the study of the interaction of animals and plants.

★ The terms *ecosystem*; *environment*; *environmental factors*.

★ How adaptation in animals and plants works.

★ How population increases and decreases, and factors limiting population growth.

★ Food chains and the relationship between predator and prey.

★ That the primary producer in a food chain is always a plant.

★ Carnivores and herbivores as different types of consumer.

★ That a food web is a set of interconnected food chains, and that decay is part of a food web.

Revision tip

Use the glossary at the back of the book for definitions of key words.

Test yourself ✓

Before moving on to the next chapter, make sure you can answer the following questions. The answers are at the back of the book.

1 Draw diagrams of typical animal and plant cells and include labels for the following: cell surface membrane, nucleus, cytoplasm, cellulose cell wall, large vacuole, chloroplasts, starch grains for storage and mitochondria.

2 What do the following words describe: tissue, organ, system?

3 Humans need a diet containing carbohydrate, fat, mineral, protein and vitamins.

   (a) (i) In a balanced diet, which one of these gives us most of our energy?

       (ii) Name a food rich in this substance.

   (b) (i) Which one of these is used mainly for growth?

       (ii) Name a food rich in this substance.

4 Complete the following sentences:

   (a) Males and females develop reproductive organs during a stage of development called _____.

   (b) The male gamete is the _____ and this is produced in the _____.

   (c) The female gamete is the _____ and this is produced in the _____.

   (d) Male and female gametes fuse together during fertilisation to form a _____.

   (e) A fertilised egg, after cell division, settles in the thick lining of the uterus wall in a process called _____.

   (f) Once the process in (e) has been completed, the mother is said to be _____.

5 List two ways in which regular exercise is an essential part of healthy living.

6 Explain what photosynthesis is.

7 What are the raw materials needed for photosynthesis?

8 What are the products of photosynthesis?

9 What happens to the oxygen produced by photosynthesis?

10 What happens to the glucose produced by photosynthesis?

11 Nitrogen is present in all proteins; magnesium is needed to make chlorophyll.

(a) Where will plants find supplies of these chemicals?

(b) Which structures enable these chemicals to enter the plants?

12 Explain what the word *variation* means.

13 Give an example of a discontinuous variation in humans and say what this results from.

14 What does a scientist mean by the word *classification*?

15 One man and his dog have much in common even though they are clearly different species. Say what they have in common in terms of biological classification.

16 Name three features that are common to all arthropods.

17 Make a table with two headings, 'vertebrate' and 'invertebrate'. Put the following animals in the correct part of your table.

earthworm   emu   shark   spider   whale
frog   crab   turtle   beetle   fox

18 What is an *ecosystem*?

19 What does the term *environment* mean?

20 What does the term *population* refer to?

21 List as many factors as you can that limit population growth.

22 Here is a simple food chain:

rose → aphid → robin → cat

(a) Which organism is the primary producer and why is it given this name?

(b) Suggest two effects on the food chain of spraying the roses with insecticide.

23 (a) What is a food web?

(b) Why is a food web different from a food chain?

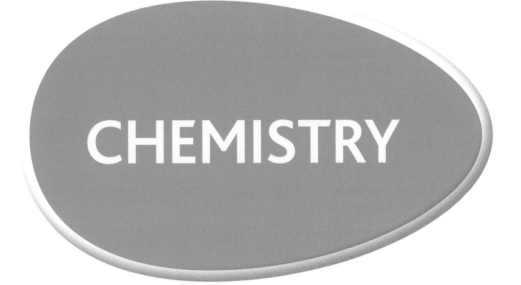

CHEMISTRY

Preliminary knowledge for 13+ Chemistry

3

→ **Revision tip**

This chapter is divided into four sections and contains material you MUST KNOW to be successful at 13+ exams.

Be sure that you can answer *all* the questions in this chapter as a first part of your revision.

3.1 Materials

Grouping and classifying materials

- The study of the materials that make up the world in which we live is called chemistry.
- Every material has two types of properties (features):
  - physical properties
  - chemical properties.

Physical properties

Physical properties are specific to substances and may be observed and/or measured without the substances changing into another substance.

Physical properties of materials include the following:

- Hardness. If *x* makes a scratch on *y*, then *x* is *harder* than *y*. For example, diamond cannot be scratched by any other substance. Hard materials keep their shape when hitting or being hit by other materials (e.g. steel hammer heads, metal golf clubs, plastic safety helmets).
- Strength. This is the ability to withstand loads without breaking or changing shape (e.g. steel for buildings and railway tracks, fibreglass for boats).
- Flexibility. How much it can be bent or twisted (e.g. wood for archery bows, string, rope, copper wire).
- Magnetic behaviour. Can it be attracted to magnets? For example, iron and steel are magnetic, while aluminium, copper and non-metals are not.
- Conductivity. **Conductors** let heat and/or electricity pass through them (e.g. all **metals**). **Insulators** do not let heat/electricity pass through them (e.g. wood, plastics, air, expanded polystyrene).

Chemical properties

Chemical properties describe the composition of a substance and how it changes into another substance. When this happens, a chemical reaction takes place.

3.2 Rocks and soils

Types of rock

There are three main types of rock, which are named after the way they are formed.

Sedimentary

These form as layers as there is a build-up of sediment, usually in the sea, rivers or lakes.

Small particles that have been weathered will be transported by water/wind and deposited in water in layers. Over a period of time more layers are deposited and the increase in pressure causes the particles to be stuck together as rock. Using a hand lens, you will see that the particles in these rocks are very small.

- Clay forms mudstone.
- Sand forms sandstone.
- Shells of creatures form limestone.

The shells of creatures that have been turned into rock over time are called fossils.

Metamorphic

These are rocks that have changed because of the action of heat and/or pressure.

- Mudstone changes into slate.
- Limestone changes into marble.

Igneous

These are rocks that are produced when molten rock (magma) cools to form crystals.

Magma rises through the Earth's crust and *cools very slowly* to form large crystals. Granite, a very hard rock, is made this way.

Some of the magma reaches the surface at a volcano and erupts as lava. The lava *cools quickly* as it comes in contact with the air or sea and forms rock made of small crystals. Most of the ocean floors are made of this type of rock, called basalt.

Types of soil

- Rocks are broken down into small particles by a process called weathering.
- Rock particles are changed into fertile soil by the addition of humus (decayed plant and animal remains that add nutrients and help keep the soil moist).
- Large rock particles have spaces between them, which allow good drainage, e.g. sandy soil.
- Tiny rock particles do not have much space between them and are easily waterlogged, e.g. clay soil.

Sandy soils – not very good for growth of most plants

- Large spaces between particles for air and water.
- Good drainage; hardly ever become waterlogged.
- Dry out quickly and minerals easily washed away.

Clay soils – not very good for growth of most plants

- Very tiny spaces between particles for air and water.
- Poor drainage; often become waterlogged.
- Lack of a good supply of air, resulting in poor root growth.
- Very little humus to provide nutrients for good plant growth.

Loam soils – ideal for good plant growth

- **Loam** is a mixture of sand and clay particles with plenty of humus.
- Good drainage – at a slower rate than in sandy soil.
- Plenty of air spaces for good root growth.
- Attracts underground animals, which helps maintain a good amount of humus.
- Retains minerals.

? **Exam-style questions**

Try these questions. The answers are given at the back of the book.

3.1 Suggest which physical property each of the following descriptions refer to and give one example of a material that fits each description.

    (a) Can be bent or twisted. (2)

    (b) Can let heat and/or electricity pass through it. (2)

    (c) Can keep its shape when hit and cannot be scratched by softer materials. (2)

    (d) Can withstand loads without breaking or changing shape. (2)

3.2 Which process breaks rocks down into smaller pieces? (1)

3.3 What do you know about the size of particles and their effect on drainage in (a) sandy soils; (b) clay soils? (2)

3.3 States of matter

Solid, liquid and gas are known as the three states of matter.

A particular amount (mass) of a substance in each of the three states will show the following features (properties):

	Solid	Liquid	Gas
Mass	Fixed	Fixed	Fixed
Volume	Fixed	Fixed	Changes
Shape	Fixed	Changes	Changes

Liquids and gases are called **fluids** because they can change shape and flow.

All matter is made up from particles, which are moving all the time.

● In a fluid the movement is from one place to another, this is called **diffusion** (see below).

● In a solid the movement is in one place in the form of **vibrations**.

Particles in solids

● Packed closely together (regular patterns in crystals).

● Held together strongly by various forces, so particles can only vibrate where they are and not move around. This is why a solid keeps its shape.

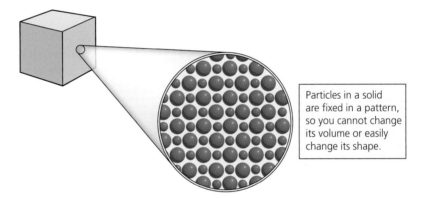

Particles in a solid are fixed in a pattern, so you cannot change its volume or easily change its shape.

Particles in liquids

● Close together, so a liquid cannot be squashed, i.e. its volume remains the same.

● Constantly moving around each other as they are not held together as strongly as in a solid, so a liquid is able to flow from one place to another.

● A liquid will change shape and match the shape of the container it is in even though the amount of liquid (volume) remains the same if it is put into different containers.

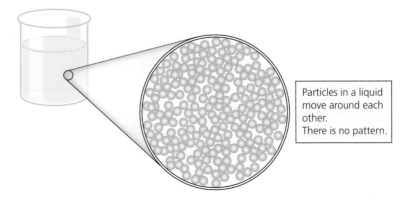

Particles in a liquid move around each other.
There is no pattern.

Particles in a gas

● Move around rapidly in all directions, so a gas will completely fill any container.

● The big spaces between particles make it relatively easy to squash a gas into a smaller space (reduce its volume). This brings the particles closer together and it is possible to squash the particles so close together that the gas becomes a liquid.

Particles bounce off the walls and each other

Particles can be squeezed closer together

Diffusion – random movement of particles in liquids and gases (fluids)

A botanist called Robert Brown noticed some pollen grains moving about in all directions in a jar of still water. As pollen grains cannot move on their own he deduced that particles of water were moving in all directions (i.e. at random) and were pushing the pollen grains.

You may have seen illuminated smoke particles being pushed around in still air, showing that gas particles move around at random.

● Random movement of particles in liquids and gases is called Brownian motion.

● Diffusion is a result of the Brownian motion and collisions between particles.

● The blue colour spreading through still water when a crystal of hydrated copper sulfate is dropped in is an example of diffusion.

> **?** **Exam-style questions**
> Try these questions. The answers are given at the back of the book.
>
> 3.4 There are three states of matter. Say what these states are and list three properties of each state. (6)
>
> 3.5 Describe (i) the position and (ii) the movement of particles in:
>
> (a) solids (2)
>
> (b) liquids (2)
>
> (c) gases (2)

3.4 Properties and changes of materials

There are two types of change.

Physical changes:

● Substances do not change into other substances, i.e. there is no chemical reaction (e.g. when salt crystals dissolve in water).

● Substances may change state (e.g. butter changes from solid to liquid as it melts).

● Changes are temporary and may be reversed (e.g. salt crystals are returned when water is evaporated or liquid butter will change to solid as it cools).

Chemical changes:

● Substances change into different substances as a result of a chemical reaction.

● In most cases the change is permanent and cannot be reversed.

Physical changes

Heating and cooling

● Adding energy to a substance makes it hotter.

● Removing energy from a substance makes it cooler.

Temperature is the measure of how hot or cold a substance is. Temperature is measured using a thermometer marked with a scale in degrees Celsius (°C). (This was originally called the centigrade scale because there are 100 degrees between the boiling and freezing points of water.)

Boiling point and melting point

The temperature at which a liquid changes into a gas is called the **boiling point**.

● The boiling point of pure water is 100°C.

● The process of changing a liquid into a gas is called **evaporation**.

● The process of changing a gas into a liquid is called **condensation**.

Evaporation and condensation can take place at any temperature – think of puddles drying up or seawater evaporating and condensing in the cooler upper air to form clouds that may eventually produce rain.

Temporary changes

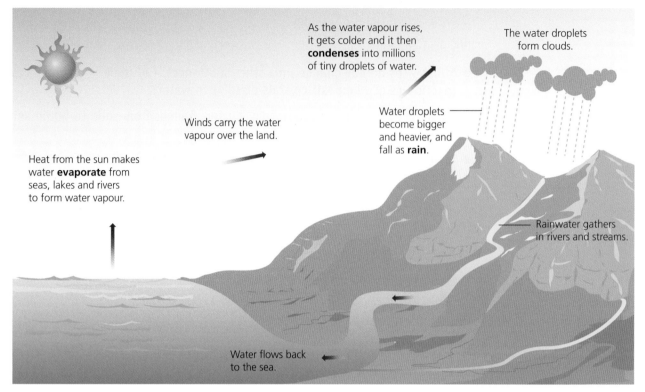

■ The water cycle: the processes of evaporation and condensation

The temperature at which a liquid changes into a solid is called the **melting point** (or freezing point).

● The freezing point of pure water is 0°C.
● The process of changing a solid into a liquid is called **melting**.
● The process of changing a liquid into a solid is called **freezing**.
● Both of these processes take place at the melting point of the substance.

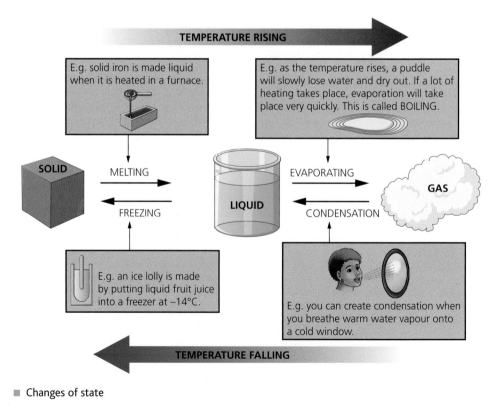

■ Changes of state

Using boiling and melting points to see if a substance is pure

- Each substance has its own boiling point and melting point.
- Adding impurities raises the boiling point and lowers the freezing points of substances. For example:
  - Adding salt to water makes it boil at a temperature higher than 100°C and freeze below 0°C. This is why salt is spread on roads when frost is forecast.
  - Water expands when it freezes (helps to break rocks into smaller pieces), but this expansion can also break water pipes, which is why motorists will add antifreeze to the water in their cars during winter and householders insulate pipes in the roof.

Chemical changes

A chemical change means a new substance has been made.

Chemical changes *not needing* heat

air (oxygen) + water + iron (solid metal) → rust (useless powder)

To stop this reaction happening, water and air (oxygen) are prevented from contact with the iron by covering it with a coat of:

- oil
- zinc (galvanising)
- paint
- plastic
- tin (as in tins containing food).

vinegar + bicarbonate of soda → fizzing + new substance + gas (carbon dioxide)

small stones + sand + cement + water → concrete (hard solid)

Chemical changes *needing* heat

- Cooking food forms new substances that cannot be changed back. For example:
  - frying/boiling an egg
  - baking dough (flour + water + yeast + sugar) to make bread.
- Burning happens when a substance is hot enough to react with oxygen (from the air) to form new substances. Burning releases more energy (heat, light, sound) than is needed to start it.

→ **Exam tip**
Heating is not the same as burning. The two are often confused, as heating can sometimes lead to burning.

Some important burning reactions are outlined below.

General reaction:

fuel + oxygen (from air) + heat → ash + gases + energy

Fossil fuels:

- Coal: a solid fuel that burns to form ash + gases + energy.
- Oil (which produces petrol, wax): a liquid that burns to form gases + energy.
- Natural gas: a gas that burns to form other gases + energy.

The reactions:

fuel (wood/coal) + oxygen + heat → ash + carbon dioxide + water + carbon (soot) + energy (heat, light)

fuel (oil/natural gas) + oxygen + heat → carbon dioxide + water + carbon (soot) + energy (heat, light)

wax (candle) + oxygen + heat → carbon dioxide + water + carbon (soot) + energy (heat, light)

Two important facts about fossil fuels:

- They are non-renewable: cannot be replaced and there is a limited supply.
- Burning causes pollution by releasing ash and gases into the air.

All fuels release carbon dioxide (a greenhouse gas) into the air.

Solid fuels, e.g. coal, release ash (as smoke) and gases (e.g. sulfur dioxide), which produce acid rain (harmful to living things).

The Bunsen burner

Two Bunsen burner has two controls:

- The air hole controls amount of air (oxygen) combining with the gas.
- The gas tap controls the amount of gas passing through the burner.

The effects of these are as follows:

Air hole	Fully closed	Half open	Fully open
Gas tap	Half on	Half on	Fully on
Type of flame	Yellow, wavy	Blue, working	Roaring
Use and characteristics of the flame	Not used for heating: not hot enough; deposits soot Silent, yellow flame	Used for gentle heating Quiet, almost invisible purple flame, with the hottest part at the tip of the flame	Used for strong heating Noisy (roaring), with the hottest part at the tip of the visible blue cone in the centre of the flame

> **? Exam-style questions**
>
> Try these questions. The answers are given at the back of the book.
>
> 3.6 In each case, give the name of the process that best describes the changes below:
>
> (a) solid → liquid (1)
>
> (b) liquid → gas (1)
>
> (c) liquid → solid (1)
>
> (d) gas → liquid (1)
>
> 3.7 The changes that are listed in question 3.6 are physical changes. List at least two features of a physical change. (2)

3.8 Pure water boils at 100°C and freezes at 0°C.

    (a) What happens to the boiling point when salt is added to water? (1)

    (b) Why do local councils often put salt on the roads in winter? (2)

3.9 (a) Iron (the only metal to rust) needs two substances to change it into rust. What are they? (2)

    (b) List three ways of preventing iron from rusting. (3)

    (c) Why is rusting not a useful chemical reaction? (2)

3.10   candle wax   coal   natural gas   oil   peat   wood

    (a) Which of the above are fossil fuels? (3)

    (b) Which of the fuels burn completely to form gases only? (3)

    (c) Which two things are needed (apart from the fuel) for it to be able to burn? (2)

    (d) Why is burning fuels harmful to the environment? (2)

Separating mixtures of materials

● Separating mixtures involves physical processes, i.e. no chemical change takes place.

● There needs to be something that one part of the mixture does that the other does not.

Mixture	Action	What happens	Physical differences
Sand + sawdust	Add water	Sand sinks; sawdust floats	Densities
Sand + iron filings	Use a magnet	Iron sticks to magnet; sand does not	Magnetic attraction
Sand + salt	Add water	Salt dissolves; sand does not	Solubility

Dissolving

● Blue copper sulfate crystals will 'disappear' in water to form a clear, blue liquid.

● We say the copper sulfate has dissolved in the water to form a blue solution.

● Substances that dissolve in liquids are called **soluble** substances.

● Substances that do not dissolve in liquids are called **insoluble** substances.

● A **solution** is a mixture of a soluble substance (called the **solute**), which is broken up and spread evenly throughout the liquid (called the **solvent**). In other words, the solvent (e.g. water) dissolves the solute (e.g. salt) to form the solution (e.g. salt solution).

● Substances will dissolve more rapidly in warm water than in cold water.

● Small crystals or powders will dissolve more easily than large crystals.

➡ **Exam tip**

If you mention that this is because of *greater surface area* available to the solvent, this will really impress the examiner.

● Mass remains the same when substances dissolve, e.g. 100 g water + 15 g salt = 115 g salt solution.

Solubility

This term describes how well a substance dissolves, i.e. how much solid dissolves in a particular amount of liquid (solvent).

- The solubility of a substance may be increased by heating
- Stirring makes a substance dissolve faster.

Sieving

- Used to separate two/more solids with different sized particles.
- A **sieve** is a tray with holes in it called a mesh. A fine mesh has small holes so will only let small particles go through it.
- Examples of sieves:
  - A tea strainer holds back the tea leaves while allowing the clear liquid to pass through.
  - A gardener will separate stones from soil by using a sieve. Stones are held in the mesh, while the smaller soil particles fall through.

Filtering

- Used to separate insoluble solids from liquids.
- Only solutions or pure liquids can *pass through* filter paper.
- **Residue:** the insoluble solid left in the filter paper, e.g. mud from muddy water.
- **Filtrate:** the liquid that passes through the filter paper, e.g. solutions and pure liquids.

Decanting is another way of separating insoluble solids from liquids.

- Insoluble solids sink and settle at the bottom of the liquid as sediment.
- Clear liquid is gently poured off, leaving the undisturbed sediment behind.

Evaporating is the *only* way of removing the solvent from a solution.

- As a solution is heated the liquid (solvent) changes into a gas (evaporates).
- When the liquid has evaporated, the dissolved solid (solute) is left behind.

? **Exam-style questions**

Try these questions. The answers are given at the back of the book.

3.11 You have a mixture of sulfur (a yellow solid) and hydrated copper sulfate (blue crystals). Sulfur is insoluble in water. Hydrated copper sulfate is soluble in water.

(a) What do the words *soluble* and *insoluble* mean? (2)

(b) What happens when you add water to your mixture? (2)

(c) If you filter the mixture after adding water, which substance is
(i) the residue; (ii) the filtrate? (2)

3.12 Copy out and complete the following sentences.

(a) A sieve is used to separate two or more _____ with _____ sized particles. (2)

(b) Filtering is used to separate _____ solids from _____. (2)

(c) Insoluble solids _____ and settle at the bottom as sediment. (1)

(d) Gently pouring off clear liquid leaving the sediment behind is called _____. (1)

3.13 Write out the following sentences, completing them by using the words listed below.

| evaporated | solute | solvent |

(a) When a solution is heated, the liquid (called the _____) changes into a gas. (1)

(b) When the liquid has _____, the _____ is left behind. (2)

★ Make sure you know

★ How materials are classified according to their physical properties.

★ The different types of rock and soil and their main features.

★ The main features of the states of matter.

★ About physical and chemical changes in materials.

★ How to separate different mixtures of materials.

> **→ Revision tip**
> Use the glossary at the back of the book for definitions of key words.

Test yourself ✓

Before moving on to the next chapter, make sure you can answer the following questions. The answers are at the back of the book.

1 (a) What do physical properties describe?

  (b) What do chemical properties describe?

2 What is humus?

3

Substance	A	B	C
Melting point (°C)	−73	−7	649
Boiling point (°C)	−10	59	1107

If room temperature is 20°C, which substance is:

(a) a solid

(b) a liquid

(c) a gas?

4 List two features of a chemical change.

5 Study the reaction:

blue powder + water → ink

Which of these three is:

(a) the solution

(b) the solvent

(c) the solute?

13+ Chemistry

4.1 The particulate nature of matter; atoms, elements and compounds

Substances – also known as matter

- All substances are made from tiny particles called **atoms**.
- There are about 100 different types of atom.
- The word 'atom' comes from the Greek word *atomos* (indivisible).
- Atoms join together to form molecules.
- Substances can be put into three main groups: solids, liquids, gases. These groups are known as the three states of matter.
- Most substances can exist in all three states; they can change from one to another by a change in temperature.
- There is no change in mass when a substance changes state.

Heating a substance causes the particles to:

- move faster, i.e. have greater kinetic energy
- move further apart, so the substance becomes bigger (increases its volume). The substance expands.

Heating a substance causes no change in mass, but increasing volume, which results in the density decreasing.

Cooling a substance causes the particles to:

- move more slowly, i.e. have less kinetic energy
- move more closely together (volume decreases).

Cooling causes no change in mass but decreasing volume, which results in the density increasing.

The expansion of liquids, e.g. mercury and alcohol, when they are heated and their contraction when they are cooled are used in thermometers.

The **melting point** is the temperature at which a:

- solid changes to a liquid
- liquid changes to a solid – also known as freezing.

The **boiling point** is the temperature at which a:

- liquid changes to a gas – i.e. evaporates
- gas changes to a liquid – i.e. condenses.

Each substance has its own boiling and melting points. This fact can be used to (i) identify a substance; (ii) determine whether it is pure or not.

Changing state

Generally, for most substances:

Adding heat: solid → liquid → gas

Removing heat (cooling): gas → liquid → solid

Sublimation

Some substances, e.g. carbon dioxide and iodine, miss out the liquid state when they are heated or cooled. This is called **sublimation**.

Adding heat: solid → gas

Removing heat (cooling): gas → solid

Types of substance

There are two main groups: pure substances and impure substances.

- Pure substances: contain *one* substance only. This group is made up of elements and compounds.
- Impure substances: contain two or more substances and are called mixtures.

Elements

- Elements are single substances that are the building blocks of all matter.
- There are about 100 elements and they are all listed in the **periodic table**.
- The smallest particle of an element is an atom of that element. The chemical symbol for each element, e.g. C for carbon, represents one atom of carbon.
- Elements are materials that are made up of one type of atom, so there are about 100 different types of atom.

Structure of atoms

> **Not examined**
> This section is not examined at Common Entrance but is included for information. Note, however, that some chemical symbols are required knowledge. Those in **bold** on the periodic table will be examined.

Every atom consists of a nucleus, which is positively charged, surrounded by a cloud of electrons, which are negatively charged.

There are three main types of particle in an atom:

(i)   Protons: positively charged particles. The number of these is called the atomic number of that element.

(ii) Neutrons: a particle found also in the nucleus that has mass but no electric charge.

(iii) Electrons: negatively charged particles with much smaller mass than protons, which move around the nucleus.

All atoms are electrically neutral, so: number of protons = number of electrons.

The periodic table

- This is a list of all the elements listed in the order of their atomic number. Note that the chemical symbols used on the periodic table represent one atom of each of the elements. The diagram below shows a small selection of those elements.

- The horizontal rows are called periods.

- The table was drawn up in 1869 by a Russian chemistry teacher called Dimitri Mendeléev.

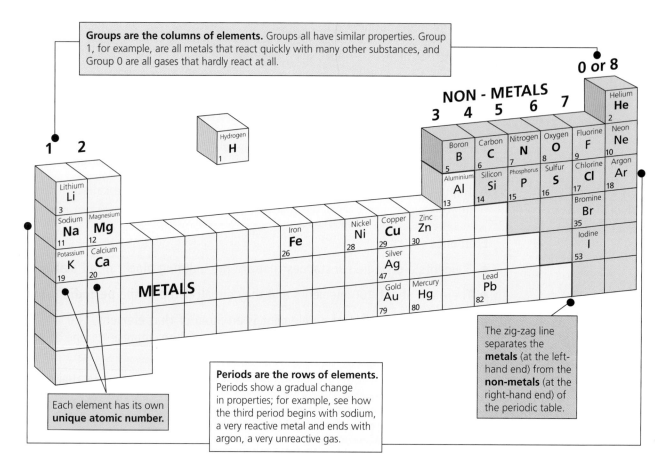

Groups are the columns of elements. Groups all have similar properties. Group 1, for example, are all metals that react quickly with many other substances, and Group 0 are all gases that hardly react at all.

Each element has its own **unique atomic number.**

Periods are the rows of elements. Periods show a gradual change in properties; for example, see how the third period begins with sodium, a very reactive metal and ends with argon, a very unreactive gas.

The zig-zag line separates the **metals** (at the left-hand end) from the **non-metals** (at the right-hand end) of the periodic table.

Metals and non-metals

Look at the periodic table and note the diagonal line towards the right that divides the table into two major groups: metals and non-metals.

Metals are:

- all solid at room temperature (except mercury – a liquid)

- shiny

- bendy – can be bent, twisted or pulled out into wires

- able to conduct electricity and heat, i.e. are conductors

- able to combine with oxygen (during burning) to form solid oxides called **bases**:

  - All bases will neutralise acids to form salts.

  - Some bases will dissolve in water to form alkalis.

Non-metals are:

- solid: carbon, iodine, silicon, sulfur
- liquid: bromine
- gas: oxygen, nitrogen, chlorine
- dull
- brittle: snap and break into powder
- able to combine with oxygen (during burning) to form oxides, which dissolve in water to form acids.

Most do not conduct electricity and heat, i.e. are insulators. Exception: carbon in the form of graphite conducts electricity.

Hydrogen – a special case

- Has physical properties of a non-metal (gas, non-conductor of electricity and heat).
- Has chemical properties of a metal (most acids are compounds of hydrogen).
- Has atomic number of 1, i.e. has a nucleus of one proton.
- Has the smallest atom and lowest density of all the elements.
- Is normally placed just outside the main body of the periodic table at the top.
- Combines with oxygen (during burning) to form a liquid oxide (water), which is neutral.

Compounds

When two or more elements combine as a result of a chemical reaction, then a compound is formed.

Compounds are *entirely different* in all respects from the elements that reacted to form them.

Compounds are represented by formulae showing the atoms that make up each **molecule**, e.g. H_2O is the formula for a water molecule, which is made from two atoms of hydrogen and one atom of oxygen.

Other important formulae are:

- CO_2 – carbon dioxide
- O_2 – oxygen gas
- CH_4 – methane
- NaCl – sodium chloride
- HCl – hydrochloric acid
- NaOH – sodium hydroxide
- $CaCO_3$ – calcium carbonate
- $CuSO_4$ – copper sulfate
- H_2SO_4 – sulfuric acid

Water vapour (variable amount in air) is:

- a neutral compound

- responsible for the humidity of the atmosphere

- a colourless liquid that freezes at 0°C and boils at 100°C – these temperatures are tests of the purity of water

- able to combine with oxygen to cause rusting of iron

- used by plants as a raw material for photosynthesis

- released into the air by (i) burning of fuels; (ii) being a waste product of respiration; (iii) evaporation of water from the sea, rivers, lakes and ponds.

A chemical test to show that water is present

Water turns white anhydrous copper sulfate blue.

> **Exam tip**
>
> This colour change tells you only that water is present, *not* that the water is pure.

Separating mixtures

Separation merely puts parts of mixtures in different places – there is no chemical reaction. The method of separation used depends upon which part of the mixture you want to keep.

Solutions

To increase the solubility of a substance:

- Heat it: the activity of molecules increases as energy is added.

- Break big chunks into smaller pieces (powder): this increases the surface area for the solvent to act upon.

- Stir it: this will increase the surface area of the solute by spreading it around.

When a substance dissolves the particles of the substance being dissolved (called the solute) are randomly distributed among the random arrangements of particles that are doing the dissolving (called the solvent). You can see this when you dissolve hydrated copper sulfate crystals in water, which disappear as a blue colour spreads throughout the clear solution.

- A solution that has the maximum amount of solute dissolved in it at a particular temperature is called a **saturated solution**. Remember that solubility increases as the temperature rises.

- Undissolved solid on the bottom of a beaker will tell you that the solution is saturated.

Methods of separation

- Sieving: separates two/more solids with different sized particles.

- Filtering: separates insoluble solids from liquids.

- Decanting: separates liquids from insoluble solids.

> **→ Exam tip**
> Only solutions and pure solvents can pass through filter paper. Insoluble solids are left as residue on the filter paper.

● Evaporating: the only way of removing the solvent from a solution – normally used to recover and keep the solute.

● Distillation: used to recover the solvent (the liquid) from a solution. This process is in two parts:

• Evaporation: to remove the solvent as a vapour from the solution.

• Condensation: to change the solvent vapour into pure solvent (the liquid).

If one liquid is recovered, the process is called simple **distillation** (see below). If two/more liquids are recovered, the process is called fractional distillation.

● Chromatography: used to separate mixtures of two or more soluble substances (see below).

Simple distillation

The water-cooled (Liebig) condenser has two main features:

● The **condensing** tube is kept cool by an outer tube containing cold water moving in the *opposite* direction from the hot vapour flow.

● The condensing tube slopes down towards the collecting tube (or flask).

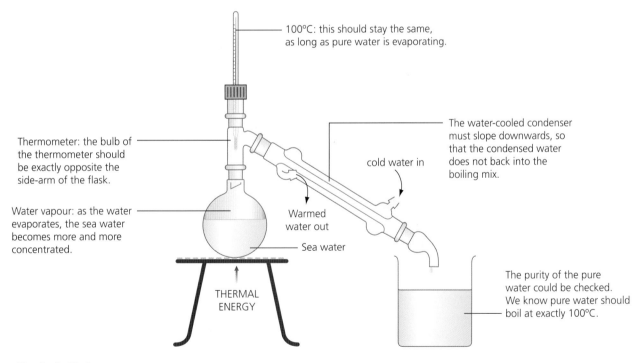

100°C: this should stay the same, as long as pure water is evaporating.

Thermometer: the bulb of the thermometer should be exactly opposite the side-arm of the flask.

The water-cooled condenser must slope downwards, so that the condensed water does not back into the boiling mix.

cold water in

Water vapour: as the water evaporates, the sea water becomes more and more concentrated.

Warmed water out

Sea water

THERMAL ENERGY

The purity of the pure water could be checked. We know pure water should boil at exactly 100°C.

■ Simple distillation

Chromatography

This method depends upon the physical property of solubility.

● Each substance has its own solubility, i.e. some solids dissolve better than others.

Water is not the only solvent you will have used, although it is the solvent used in most writing inks. You might have used ethanol or propanone to extract the green colour from leaves and dry cleaners will use special solvents to remove grease stains from clothes.

● The solvent will move up chromatography paper (like filter paper) and will take the dissolved solids with it.

● The chromatography paper tries to absorb the solids and 'hold them back'.

● Solids will stop at some point on the paper, while the solvent continues to travel upwards.

● The solid that dissolves best, travels the furthest, i.e. stops at the highest point on the paper.

● Chromatography is used for analysis of small quantities of mixtures. It will often be used by:

  • food chemists – to determine the additives and ingredients in foodstuffs, e.g. the colourings in sweets

  • police – to match up samples from a suspect to substances found at a crime scene

  • biochemists – to separate proteins into their various parts in the constant search for drugs to cure illnesses.

? Exam-style questions

Try these questions. The answers are given at the back of the book.

4.1 Make a table with the headings *elements*, *compounds* and *mixtures*.

Put the following substances into the correct columns: (12)

air	carbon	carbon dioxide	distilled water
sea water	iron filings	crude oil	dilute sulfuric acid
magnesium	oxygen	sodium chloride	iron sulfide

4.2 Make a table with three headings *metal element*, *non-metal element* and *compound*. Put the following substances into the correct part of your table: (10)

carbon	copper sulfate	iron filings	magnesium	mercury
oxygen	sodium	sulfur	water	zinc oxide

4.3 Select the 'odd one out' in each of the following groups and suggest why you have made this choice.

(a) Copper, iron, mercury, zinc. (2)

(b) Copper, iron, lead, sodium. (2)

(c) Carbon dioxide, copper oxide, nitrogen oxide, sulfur dioxide. (2)

(d) Carbon, iron, sulfur, zinc. (2)

4.4 *Heating* a substance can cause a *chemical reaction* to take place. For example, a *reactant* may *decompose* into two *products*. What do the words in italics mean? (5)

4.5 (a) What evidence would you look for to show that a combining reaction had taken place? (2)

(b) Choose an example of a combining reaction and write a word equation that describes this. (4)

4.6 Dry air has the following composition:

- 78% gas A

- 20% gas B

- 2% other gases

    (a) What is:

        (i)   gas A?

        (ii) gas B?   (1)

    (b) Name one of the other gases.   (1)

    (c) (i)   What is the gas that is responsible for the humidity of the air?   (1)

        (ii) Describe a chemical test to identify this gas.   (2)

4.7 Copy out the table and complete it to suggest whether the processes listed cause the amounts of nitrogen, oxygen and carbon dioxide to increase, decrease or remain the same.   (15)

Process	Nitrogen	Oxygen	Carbon dioxide
Burning a fossil fuel			
Photosynthesis			
Respiration			
Passing air through limewater			
Rusting			

4.8 (a) Draw a labelled diagram to show how you would *best* obtain some pure water from a sample of sea water.   (6)

    (b) How would you test that the water you had obtained was pure?   (2)

4.9 What method would you use to:

    (a) Recover solid salt from salt solution?   (1)

    (b) Recover mud from muddy water?   (1)

    (c) Find out how many pigments there were in black felt-tipped pen ink?   (1)

4.3 Indicators, acids and alkalis

Indicators

These are substances that change their appearance (e.g. colour) when they come in contact with particular substances.

They *indicate* that a particular substance is present.

Indicators you know about already

- Limewater: changes from clear to chalky to show carbon dioxide is present.

- Anhydrous copper sulfate: changes from white to blue to show water is present.

Indicators to show that liquids are either acid or alkali, or neutral

Litmus is extracted from a type of lichen plant and forms a purple solution in water.

- Purple litmus solution will turn red when it is added to acids.
- Purple litmus solution will turn blue when it is added to alkalis.

Litmus is used in the laboratory in three different forms:

- As a purple solution of the dye in water.
- As red test papers to detect alkalis and neutral liquids.
- As blue test papers to detect acids and neutral liquids.

Testing 'strength' of acids/alkalis – the pH scale

The **pH scale** runs from 0 to 14.

- The middle of the scale is 7 and all liquids with a pH of 7 are neutral.
- Solutions that have a pH less than 7 are acids.
- Solutions that have a pH more than 7 are alkalis.
- Weak acids/alkalis have pH values close to the mid-point (7). For example, a range of 5–9 includes:
  - 'natural' acids found in foods: vinegar, citrus fruits (pH 5–7)
  - 'weak' alkalis such as detergents, medicine to cure indigestion, baking powder (pH 7–9).
- Strong acids/alkalis have pH values close to the end points (0 and 14). For example:
  - sulfuric, hydrochloric acids (pH 0–4)
  - sodium, calcium hydroxides (pH 10–14).

pH values can be determined by using either a **universal indicator** or a pH probe.

Universal indicator (UI)

This is a mixture of plant dyes and is available as a green liquid or as test papers. The indicator will change colour for different pH values.

pH scale

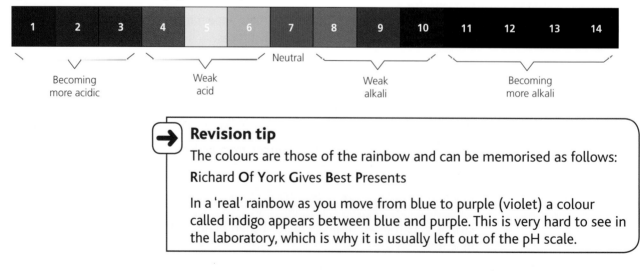

pH scale (a scale of numbers ranging from 1 to 14).

> ### → Revision tip
> The colours are those of the rainbow and can be memorised as follows:
> **Richard Of York Gives Best Presents**
>
> In a 'real' rainbow as you move from blue to purple (violet) a colour called indigo appears between blue and purple. This is very hard to see in the laboratory, which is why it is usually left out of the pH scale.

Neutralisation

Acids are able to 'cancel' out alkalis in a chemical reaction known as **neutralisation**.

For example, sodium hydroxide is a strong alkali – purple with UI added. Hydrochloric acid (hydrogen chloride) is a strong acid – red with UI added. Add the acid slowly to the alkali until the neutral point is reached – UI turns green.

The resulting solution will be (i) warmer; (ii) a neutral solution of sodium chloride (a salt), dissolved in water.

The word equation to describe the chemical reaction that has happened is:

hydrochloric acid + sodium hydroxide → sodium chloride + water

acid   +   alkali   →   salt   + water

The water can be evaporated from the sodium chloride solution to leave crystals of solid sodium chloride.

● Lime is an alkali that is used to treat acid soils, acid indigestion and to manufacture fertiliser.

Diluting acids with water

● Adding water to acids does not substantially change the pH of the acid – it merely dilutes the acid.

● Concentrated acids are made dilute by slowly adding small quantities of concentrated acid to large quantities of water.

More about salts

Acids

These are all compounds of hydrogen and it is the acid that gives a salt its second name.

Name of acid	Chemical name	Second name of salts produced
Hydrochloric acid	Hydrogen chloride	...chloride
Sulfuric acid	Hydrogen sulfate	...sulfate
Nitric acid	Hydrogen nitrate	...nitrate
Carbonic acid	Hydrogen carbonate	...carbonate

Alkalis

All metal oxides are called bases.

Alkalis are bases that are soluble in water and are named hydroxides.

Base	Soluble in water	Alkali formed	'Common name'
Calcium oxide	Yes	Calcium hydroxide	Lime
Copper oxide	No	–	–
Iron oxide	No	–	–
Potassium oxide	Yes	Potassium hydroxide	Caustic potash
Sodium oxide	Yes	Sodium hydroxide	Caustic soda
Zinc oxide	No	–	–

When a base neutralises an acid, the first name of the base becomes the first name of the salt.

acid + base → salt + water

For example:

copper oxide + sulfuric acid → copper sulfate + water

iron oxide + sulfuric acid → iron sulfate + water

Carbonates can make salts

All carbonates produce carbon dioxide when added to acids – they also neutralise acids to form salts.

acid + carbonate → salt + water + carbon dioxide

sulfuric acid + copper carbonate → copper sulfate + water + carbon dioxide

Some metals make salts

Some metals react with acids. When they do, salts are formed and the gas given off is hydrogen.

acid + metal → salt + hydrogen

For example:

sulfuric acid + zinc → zinc sulfate + hydrogen

About hydrogen

- The least dense of all gases – not found in our atmosphere.

- A colourless gas that burns explosively in air to form water.

- Test with a lighted splint – a test tube of hydrogen will burn with a yellow flame and sometimes a 'squeaky pop' will be heard.

? Exam-style questions

Try these questions. The answers are given at the back of the book.

4.10 What colour will blue litmus paper go when put into the following liquids? (5)

hydrochloric acid   limewater   sodium hydroxide   sugar solution   water

4.11 Draw a pH scale running from 0 to 14. On your diagram label:

(a) The neutral point. (1)

(b) Acids – showing strongest and weakest. (2)

(c) Alkalis – showing strongest and weakest. (2)

4.12 Copy out and complete the following:

(a) Acid + base → _____ + water (1)

(b) Acid + alkali → _____ + water (1)

(c) Acid + carbonate → _____ + water + _____ (2)

(d) Acid + metal → _____ + _____ (2)

(e) Adding acid to an alkali _____ the pH of the mixture. (1)

(f) Neutralising an acid by a base _____ the pH of the mixture. (1)

(g) Adding water to an acid _____ the pH of the acid. (1)

4.4 Chemical reactions involving oxygen

Chemical test to identify oxygen

Oxygen is the *only* colourless gas that re-lights a glowing splint.

Preparation of oxygen

- Thermal **decomposition** of potassium permanganate. This decomposes according to the word equation:

  potassium permanganate (s) + heat $\rightarrow$ oxygen (g) + residue (s)

  You are not expected to name the residue at this stage.

- Decomposition of hydrogen peroxide:

  hydrogen peroxide (l) $\rightarrow$ oxygen (g) + water (l)

  This reaction is so slow that manganese oxide is added to speed up the reaction. At the end of the reaction, manganese oxide may be recovered. Manganese oxide is called a **catalyst** because it speeds up the reaction without being changed itself.

Reactions of oxygen

Oxygen and reactions with elements

- When magnesium burns in air, white magnesium oxide is formed.
- When copper is heated in air, there is no burning but black copper oxide is formed.

In both cases, a combining reaction has taken place as each metal combines with oxygen. The combining reaction is called **oxidation**.

- Oxidation is a chemical reaction that involves combination with oxygen.
- When an element is oxidised, only one product is formed.

> **Exam tip**
> If an exam question says 'heated in a plentiful supply of air', this is another way of saying there is the opportunity of combining with oxygen.

Oxygen and reactions with compounds

When a candle burns in air, the two products carbon dioxide and water are produced. So we know that a candle is not an element, but contains at least two substances.

candle (s) + oxygen (g) $\rightarrow$ water (g) + carbon dioxide (g)

- The hydrogen in the water must have come from the candle.
- The carbon in the gas must have come from the candle.

Looking at the word equation tells us that apart from the oxygen, no other substances are involved.

Candle wax is a compound that contains only hydrogen and carbon. Compounds that contain *only* hydrogen and carbon are called **hydrocarbons**.

hydrocarbon + oxygen → energy (heat and light) + water + carbon dioxide

Hydrocarbons are found in the many products of crude oil, e.g. petrol, candle wax, polythene and some plastics.

Oxygen and fuels

Fuels are substances that we burn with the purpose of using the excess heat energy that is released by the reaction with oxygen.

All fuels have the following in common:

● Fuels by themselves do not release energy. It is the fuel/oxygen reaction that releases energy.

● Most fuels contain carbon compounds. This means that when they burn, carbon dioxide is released into the atmosphere. The exception to this is hydrogen, which produces water vapour when it burns.

Fuels include:

● living fuels – wood and materials from plants

● semi-fossil fuels – e.g. peat

● fossil fuels – coal, oil, gas. These are fuels formed from the dead remains of animals and plants that lived millions of years ago.

Burning coal

● Coal contains compounds of both carbon and sulfur.

● When coal is burnt, both gases, carbon dioxide and sulfur dioxide, are released into the atmosphere.

● Sulfur dioxide dissolves in the water of the atmosphere to form acid rain.

Burning gas

● Natural gas is the hydrocarbon methane. If your laboratory is connected to the gas supply, this is the gas that supplies your Bunsen burners.

Burning oil

● Nearly all forms of transport burn some form of hydrocarbon as a fuel.

● Hydrocarbons come from crude oil that has been separated into its various compounds by fractional distillation at a refinery.

● Incomplete burning of petrol causes carbon monoxide (a poisonous gas) to be released.

● As carbon monoxide leaves the exhaust pipe, it combines with the oxygen in the air to form carbon dioxide.

Oxygen and rusting

The term rusting refers *only* to the corrosion of iron.

Air — Nail — Calcium chloride	Oil — Nail — Water boiled to remove oxygen and cooled to room temperature	Nail — Water	Nail — Warm water (50°C)
No water	No air	Air and water (control)	Air and warm water
No rust	No rust	Rusty	Very rusty

Rusting occurs when iron is exposed to oxygen and water. You may remember putting some wet iron wool in a measuring cylinder and inverting this over water. After a time the iron has rusted and the water has risen up the inside of the cylinder. When the reaction stops – after a few days – you will see that 20% of the air has been used up (similar to the 20% used up when burning a candle in a bell jar), showing the involvement of oxygen in rusting.

Rusting costs money:

● to replace items that have rusted

● to take measures to prevent rusting from taking place.

There are three ways of preventing iron from rusting:

● Exclude oxygen and water by covering with a layer of grease, oil, paint or plastic.

● Exclude oxygen and water by covering the iron with a less reactive metal, e.g. tin.

● Coat the iron with a more reactive metal, e.g. zinc. This process is called galvanising. The zinc reacts with the water and oxygen instead of the iron, i.e. is sacrificed to spare the iron. This form of prevention is called sacrificial protection.

? Exam-style questions

Try these questions. The answers are given at the back of the book.

4.13 What does the word *oxidation* mean? (2)

4.14 Methane is a hydrocarbon.

(a) What is a hydrocarbon? (1)

(b) Which two products are formed when methane burns? (2)

(c) Write a word equation to describe the burning of methane. (4)

4.15 Coal is a fossil fuel that burns well in air.

(a) What is meant by the term *fossil fuel*? (1)

(b) Name two other fossil fuels. (2)

(c) (i) Other than water vapour name two gases released when coal burns in air. (2)

(ii) Suggest what happens to both of these gases when they come into contact with water vapour in the air. (2)

4.16 (a) Why is rusting said to be one of the most expensive
chemical reactions? (2)

(b) Name three substances involved in rusting. (3)

(c) Describe three ways that help to prevent rusting taking place. (3)

4.5 Chemical reactions comparing the reactivity of some elements

Metals are placed in order according to how well they react with oxygen, water, steam and acids in what is called the **reactivity series**.

Reacting metals with oxygen

- Sodium and potassium react so well with oxygen that they have to be stored under oil. Both are soft metals and, when cut, their shiny surfaces quickly become dull as the metals react with the oxygen in the air.

- Gold does not react with oxygen – think of ancient Egyptian treasures that are still shiny after exposure to air (oxygen) for thousands of years.

Burning metals

Metal	Result of burning
Sodium/potassium	Reacts with oxygen without burning
Calcium	Burns with a fierce red flame
Magnesium	Burns with a brilliant white flame
Zinc	Burns with a bright, fierce blue/green flame
Iron	Burns with yellow sparks
Copper	Very hard to burn – small green flame is produced
Gold	Does not burn at all

Reacting metals with water

Metals that do so, react with water according to the word equation:

metal (s) + water (l) → metal hydroxide (l) + hydrogen (g)

Look for:

- bubbles of hydrogen gas

- formation of metal hydroxide: indicator shows alkali is present.

The following metals are added to water that has universal indicator added:

- Potassium: whizzes round; bursts into purple flame; hydrogen is given off; water changes to purple as potassium hydroxide is produced.

- Sodium: whizzes round; becomes hot enough to melt itself; hydrogen is given off; water changes to purple as sodium hydroxide is produced.

- Calcium: sinks; rapid bubbles of hydrogen appear; water changes to purple as calcium hydroxide is produced.

- Magnesium, zinc, iron: these reactions are very slow in cold water as shown by universal indicator taking a long time to change from green to purple, so reactions are speeded up by using steam.

Reacting metals with steam

metal (s) + steam (g) → metal oxide (s) + hydrogen (g)

Look for:

● production of the metal oxide

● production of hydrogen – this will burn with a yellow flame. At the end of the apparatus there is a tube that lets the gases produced escape. The flame can be seen at the end of the tube.

Metal	Action of water	Action of steam
Potassium, sodium, calcium	React to form metal hydroxide and hydrogen	Too violent and dangerous
Magnesium, zinc, iron	Very slow reaction	React to form metal oxide plus hydrogen
Copper	No reaction	No reaction

Position of hydrogen in the series

iron + water (hydrogen oxide) → iron oxide + hydrogen

● Iron has taken the oxygen away from the water and has itself been oxidised to form iron oxide.

● The process of removal of oxygen by another substance is called **reduction**.

● The substance that does the taking away is called a reducing agent.

In this case, iron is the reducing agent that reduces water to hydrogen.

Look at the table above:

● Iron is able to reduce water to hydrogen – so iron is higher than hydrogen in the reactivity series.

● Copper is not able to reduce water – so copper is lower than hydrogen in the reactivity series.

Reacting metals with dilute acids

All acids are compounds of hydrogen.

metal + acid → salt + hydrogen

For example:

magnesium + sulfuric acid → magnesium sulfate + hydrogen

So an acid is a compound containing hydrogen, which can be replaced by a metal that is higher than hydrogen in the reactivity series.

Metal	Action of cold dilute acid	Action of warm dilute acid
Potassium, sodium	Too violent and dangerous	Too violent and dangerous
Calcium, magnesium, zinc, iron	Reacts to form salt and hydrogen	Too violent and dangerous
Tin, lead	No reaction	Reacts to form salt and hydrogen
Copper	No reaction	No reaction

Displacing metals from salts

If you put an iron nail into some copper sulfate solution, after a time:

● the solution loses its blue colour

● the nail becomes coated with copper.

Iron, being higher than copper in the reactivity series, has displaced copper from copper sulfate solution.

iron (s) + copper sulfate (l) → iron sulfate (l) + copper (s)

Metal	Reaction with magnesium chloride solution	Reaction with iron nitrate solution	Reaction with lead chloride solution	Reaction with copper sulfate solution
Magnesium	✗	✓	✓	✓
Zinc	✗	✓	✓	✓
Iron	✗	✗	✓	✓
Lead	✗	✗	✗	✓
Copper	✗	✗	✗	✗

Reacting metals with oxides

Look at part of the reactivity series:

magnesium
zinc
iron
copper

- Magnesium will react with: zinc oxide, iron oxide, copper oxide.
- Iron will react with only copper oxide.
- Copper could not react with any of the oxides of iron, zinc or magnesium.
- The reaction between copper oxide and magnesium is very vigorous (products are 'blown away' in the reaction, leaving very little in the crucible).
- The reaction between copper oxide and iron is gentle (a red glow spreads through the mixture).

These results show that the further apart the two metals are in the reactivity series, the more violent will be the reaction.

Carbon in the reactivity series

Consider the following reactions you will have carried out in the laboratory.

carbon + magnesium oxide → no reaction

So magnesium is more reactive than carbon.

carbon + zinc oxide → no reaction

So zinc is more reactive than carbon, at temperatures that can be produced by a Bunsen flame (750–800°C). (In fact, carbon *will* reduce zinc oxide, but at a temperature of over 1000°C.)

carbon + iron oxide → iron + carbon dioxide

So carbon is more reactive than iron (this reaction is important in the industrial production of iron).

Carbon can now be placed just above iron but below zinc in the reactivity series.

> **? Exam-style questions**
>
> Try these questions. The answers are given at the back of the book.
>
> **4.17** What is meant by the 'reactivity series' of metals? (1)
>
> **4.18** What do the following words mean: oxidation; reduction? (4)

4.19 Given the following order of reactivity – magnesium, zinc, iron, copper – for each of the following pairs write a word equation for any reaction that does take place.

    (a) zinc + magnesium oxide (2)

    (b) zinc + copper oxide (2)

    (c) magnesium + iron oxide (2)

    (d) iron + copper sulfate (2)

    (e) iron + magnesium sulfate (2)

    (f) zinc + iron sulfate (2)

4.20 You have four metals A, B, C and D. You find out that:

    • B reduces C oxide when they are heated.

    • There is no reaction when B is heated with D oxide.

    • There is no reaction when A is heated with C oxide.

    Put the metals in order of reactivity (most reactive first). (4)

4.21 Copper carbonate was heated in air. It lost mass and a black powder was left as a residue.

    (a) **(i)** What was the black powder? (1)

        (ii) Write a word equation to show how the black powder can be changed to copper by heating it with carbon. (4)

    (b) The black powder is added to warm dilute sulfuric acid. A blue solution is formed.

        (i) What effect will the black powder have on the pH of the acid? (1)

        (ii) What would you add to the solution to obtain some copper? (1)

4.22 Iron is extracted from iron oxide by heating it with carbon in a blast furnace. Write a word equation for this chemical reaction. (4)

4.6 Chemical reactions and the extraction of metals from minerals

A few unreactive metals (gold, silver, copper) can be found as metals.

Most metals are found as a mixture of rock and metal compound (mineral), which we call an **ore**.

Extraction of metals

The method of extraction will depend upon the reactivity of the metal.

The higher a metal is in the reactivity series, the harder it is to extract it from its ore.

Extraction of copper

A source of copper is the mineral malachite (copper carbonate).

Extraction of copper from malachite is in two stages:

1   Making the oxide

        copper carbonate + heat → copper oxide + carbon dioxide

2   Reducing the oxide by heating with carbon

copper oxide + carbon → copper + carbon dioxide

Extraction of iron

- The main ore is haematite (iron oxide) – a mixture of rock and iron oxide.
- The raw materials (called the charge) that are put into the top of a furnace, which heats them at a high temperature, are:
  - iron ore – the source of iron
  - limestone – to combine with the rock to form slag
  - coke – the supply of carbon.
- There are two main reactions that happen in the extraction of iron from its ore:
  - removal of oxygen from iron oxide to leave iron
  - formation of slag to remove the rock from the iron ore.

Carbon as coke is heated to produce carbon monoxide. Carbon monoxide reduces iron oxide and the iron formed is molten at the high temperature (1800°C) produced. This runs to the bottom of the furnace where it collects until it is tapped (run off).

iron oxide + carbon monoxide → iron + carbon dioxide

The 'rocky' part of the iron ore will be mainly composed of sandy substances such as silicon oxide. This will combine with the calcium oxide (produced by heating the limestone) to form slag. Slag will be molten and so drips to the bottom of the furnace where it floats on the more dense iron.

sandy rock (silicon oxide) + calcium oxide → slag (calcium silicate)

Extraction of aluminium

- Extraction requires a large supply of electricity and high temperatures.
- The main mineral source is bauxite (aluminium oxide).
- Bauxite is purified chemically and is dissolved in molten cryolite. The cryolite lowers the temperature at which the ore melts (otherwise the furnace temperature would need to be over 2000°C) and the solution has an electric current passed through it to extract the aluminium metal.

Limestone

- Calcium carbonate is the main compound in limestone.
- Limestone is a sedimentary rock made by the decomposition of the shells of creatures that lived in the ancient seas.

Uses of limestone

Building	Used as 'bricks' for houses; although they look good, they are prone to attack from acid rain over the years
Extraction of iron	Used in the extraction of iron from its ore.
Manufacture of cement	The basic ingredient in two important substances used in the construction industry: mortar (the 'glue' that binds bricks together) and cement (an important part of concrete)
Manufacture of lime	An alkali that is used by farmers and growers to neutralise acid soils

Exam-style questions

Try these questions. The answers are given at the back of the book.

4.23 Bronze is an alloy (mixture) of copper and tin. Explain why knowledge of chemistry will help you to remember that the Bronze Age came before the Iron Age. (3)

4.24 Iron is higher in the reactivity series than lead. The main ore of lead is galena (lead sulfide) and lead oxide reacts with carbon.

    (a) Write a word equation to show how you change galena into lead oxide. (5)

    (b) Write a word equation for the reaction with lead oxide. (5)

    (c) Would iron react with lead oxide? Give a reason. (2)

4.25 Iron is extracted from iron oxide using materials heated to a high temperature.

    (a) What are the three solid materials used in the extraction of iron and what is the purpose of each material? (6)

    (b) What substance removes the oxygen from iron oxide to make iron? (1)

    (c) Write a word equation to describe the reaction of iron oxide with carbon monoxide. (4)

4.26 Below is a table that tells you about the extraction of three metals.

Metal	Extraction
Aluminium	From aluminium oxide by a chemical reaction involving large amounts of electricity
Gold	By crushing the ore and washing it
Iron	From iron oxide by a chemical reaction with carbon

    (a) Put the three metals in order of increasing reactivity. (3)

    (b) Aluminium is more expensive than iron even though it is more abundant. Why is this? (2)

    (c) Why is gold much more expensive than aluminium? (2)

★ Make sure you know

★ How substances can be classified and how they can change state.

★ The differences between pure and impure substances.

★ The main features of the periodic table.

★ How to separate mixtures.

★ How indicators are used to identify particular substances.

★ The main features of salts.

★ The main features of oxygen and how it reacts with different elements and compounds.

★ How metals react with different substances.

★ The main features of unreactive metals and minerals.

Revision tip

Use the glossary at the back of the book for definitions of key words.

Before moving on to the next chapter, make sure you can answer the following questions. The answers are at the back of the book.

1 (a) What is an element?

   (b) Approximately, how many elements are there?

   (c) Where can you find a list of all known elements?

   (d) What is significant about the atoms of elements?

2 List two important features of all chemical reactions.

3 (a) What does an indicator do?

   (b) Name four indicators and say what they are used for.

4 What will you observe when red litmus is added to each of the following?

   (a) hydrochloric acid

   (b) limewater

   (c) sodium hydroxide

   (d) sugar solution

   (e) water

5 How would you test a gas to show that it is oxygen?

6 Write word equations that describe what happens when the following burn in a plentiful supply of air:

   (a) carbon

   (b) magnesium

   (c) sulfur

7 Write a word equation for each of the reactions described below:

   (a) An iron nail becomes pink if placed in copper sulfate solution.

   (b) Copper foil becomes pale grey if placed in silver nitrate solution.

8 What is an ore?

9 Aluminium, copper, glass, iron, lead, plastic, rubber. From this list, choose one that would be the most suitable for the uses given below. In each case, give a reason for your choice.

   (a) a picnic mug

   (b) the inner wires of an electric cable

   (c) the guttering round the roof of a house

   (d) a bucket to carry red hot ashes

   (e) wings of an aeroplane

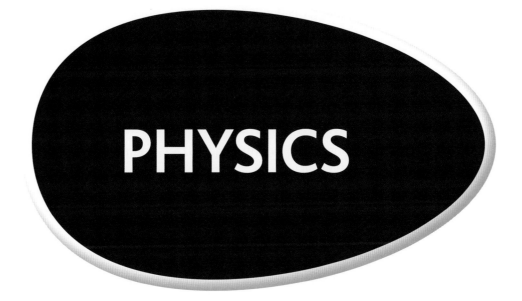

Preliminary knowledge for 13+ Physics

> **Revision tip**
>
> This chapter is divided into four sections and contains material you MUST KNOW to be successful at 13+ exams.
>
>   Be sure that you can answer ALL the questions in this chapter as a first part of your revision.

5.1 Simple electric circuits

- Lamps light, motors turn and buzzers sound when an electric current passes through them.
- We say that electric current moves from the + (positive) terminal through the **circuit** to the − (negative) terminal of a cell/battery. (This is called the conventional flow of current.)
- A battery is made up of two or more cells connected together.
- Electric current moves through wires (leads), which are electrical conductors.

Remember from your study of chemistry about conductivity:

- Conductors let heat and/or electricity pass through them.

   For example, all metals.

- Insulators do not let heat/electricity pass through them.

   For example, wood, plastics, air, expanded polystyrene.

For an electric circuit to work:

- there must be no gaps, i.e. there must be a complete circuit
- all cells must face the same way, i.e. be the same way round.

Drawing electric circuits

- Circuits should be drawn as straight lines for the conducting wires.
- Circuit symbols should be drawn to represent the various components (lamps, cells, etc.).

Circuit symbols

Component	Symbol	What the component is used for
Cell (battery)	—|⊢—	Provides electrical energy for the circuit
Power supply (lab pack)	—o o—	Alternative to using cells
Wire (lead)	———	Lets electric current travel through it
Bulb/lamp	—⊗—	Converts electrical energy into heat and light energy
Motor	—(M)—	Converts electrical energy into movement energy
Buzzer	—⊲	Converts electrical energy into **sound energy**
Push-button switch	—•—o o—	When pressed, it completes the circuit, allowing the current to flow
Switch	—o⁄o—	When closed, it completes the circuit, allowing the current to flow

Adding cells or lamps

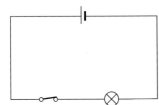

- The lamp, cell and switch are connected in series – the components are connected one after another. And there is only one path for the current to follow.

- The lamp is said to shine with 'normal brightness' (one cell, one lamp).

- Adding more lamps makes each lamp dimmer.

- Adding another cell makes the lamp in the circuit brighter.

In general

- If the number of cells = the number of lamps, the lamps are of normal brightness.

- If the number of cells > the number of lamps, the lamps are brighter than normal brightness.

- If the number of cells < the number of lamps, the lamps are dimmer than normal brightness.

The misnamed 'short circuit'

- This is misnamed because it has nothing to do with length.

- Electric current will always take the easiest route.

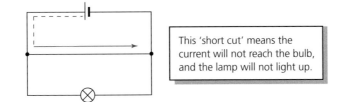

This 'short cut' means the current will not reach the bulb, and the lamp will not light up.

A fault in mains equipment could cause a person to receive an electric shock. To prevent this, an earth wire is found in most plugs. The earth wire is the short circuit that takes the current to the ground rather than passing through a person.

Fuse

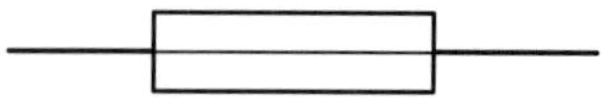

Used as a safety device to protect components from damage caused by high currents.

How a fuse works

When there is a current in a circuit that is too high for the fuse, the fuse wire heats – melts – and breaks the circuit, stopping all current in the circuit immediately.

5.2 Forces and magnets

What is a force?

● A **force** is an invisible push or pull – you can only see what a force does.

● A force can:

  • make a stationary object move

  • make a moving object go faster or slower

  • make a moving object change direction

  • make a moving object stop

  • change the shape of an object.

Key facts about forces

● All forces (i) have size; (ii) act in one direction only.

● We measure the size of a force in **newtons** (N) using a newton meter (newton spring balance).

● We show the direction and size of a force by drawing arrows:

  • large arrow – large force

  • small arrow – small force

● Forces act in pairs in opposite directions.

- When the forces are equal, the forces are balanced – no change in movement happens.
- If one force is bigger than the other, the forces are unbalanced – movement happens in the same direction as the larger force acts.
- When a force acts, the other force of the pair acting in the opposite direction is called the reaction force.

Types of force

Magnetic forces

- A freely suspended **magnet** will always have the same end pointing towards the magnetic North Pole, so this end is called the north-seeking pole. The other end is called the south-seeking pole.
- At present, magnetic north pole is close to the geographical North Pole.
- A compass needle is a small magnet.
- Only materials containing iron (e.g. steel) will be **attracted** by a magnet – such materials are called magnetic.
- Magnetic force can work at a distance, e.g. action of a compass needle, whereas pushing a door open requires direct contact.

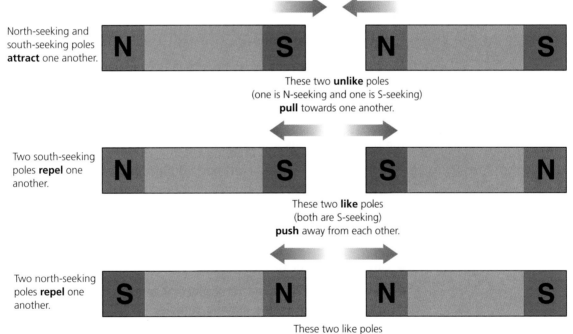

North-seeking and south-seeking poles **attract** one another.

These two **unlike** poles
(one is N-seeking and one is S-seeking)
pull towards one another.

Two south-seeking poles **repel** one another.

These two **like** poles
(both are S-seeking)
push away from each other.

Two north-seeking poles **repel** one another.

These two like poles
(both are N-seeking)
push away from each other.

■ How magnets behave

Gravitational force

- **Gravity** is the force of attraction between any masses.
- Gravity never pushes – it only pulls.
- The size of gravitational force depends upon:
  - the mass of the object
  - the distance between the centre of each object.

How light travels

● Light travels very fast – nothing yet has been found to travel faster.

● Light rays travel in straight lines – you cannot see round corners.

● Light rays travel through some materials:

  • **Transparent** materials, e.g. glass, water. Light rays will pass through these materials and you can see clear images through them.

  • **Translucent** materials, e.g. tracing paper, some plastics. Some light rays are changed as they pass through these materials, which means that you cannot see a clear image of what is on the other side.

  • **Opaque** materials, e.g. wood, metal, pottery. Light rays cannot pass through these materials at all. Such materials block light rays and form **shadows**.

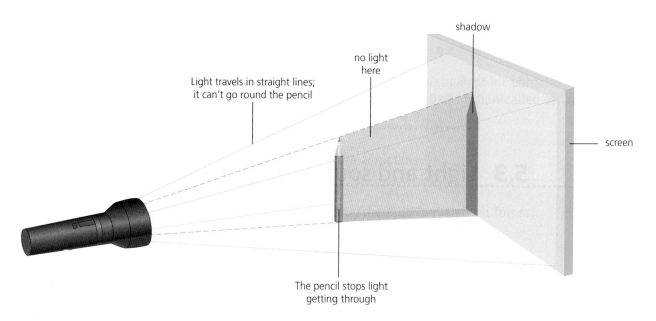

shadow

no light here

Light travels in straight lines; it can't go round the pencil

screen

The pencil stops light getting through

■ Looking at shadows

● To make the shadow larger: (i) move the pencil closer to the light source, or (ii) move the screen further away from the pencil.

● To make the shadow smaller: (i) move the pencil away from the light source, or (ii) move the screen closer to the pencil.

● The sharp outlines of the shadow of the pencil confirm that light travels in straight lines.

Reflection of light

● Shiny surfaces, e.g. mirrors, bounce light rays off the surface at the same angle as they hit the mirror surface. This is called **reflection**.

● Rough surfaces, e.g. paper, stone, cloth, reflect light rays in many directions – the light has been **scattered**.

Sound

● When a guitar string is plucked, it moves backwards and forwards, i.e. it vibrates.

● Each vibration causes the surrounding air to be squashed and stretched in pulses and so sound waves are formed.

- Vibrations cause sound waves to be produced.

- When sound waves meet our eardrum, similar vibrations are set up in our ear. These vibrations are changed into messages in the ear, which are sent to the brain, so we hear the sound of the guitar string.

- Sound waves need something to stretch and squash, so they are able to travel through solids and liquids as well as air and other gases.

There are no particles at all in a **vacuum** (nothing to squash and stretch), so sound cannot travel through a vacuum.

There is a famous demonstration that you may have seen of an alarm clock ringing its bell while it is inside a bell jar. As the air is removed by a vacuum pump the ringing becomes quieter. When all the air is removed, there is no sound at all even though you can see the hammer on the clock is still hitting the bell.

Loudness

- **Loudness** depends upon the energy of the vibration, i.e. how hard something is plucked or hit.

- More energy used in the hitting/plucking results in larger vibrations, which produce louder sounds.

Pitch

- **Pitch** describes how high or low a sound is.

- Pitch is determined by the:

  - length of vibrating material. Shortening a vibrating string increases the pitch of a sound. Shortening the string makes the vibrations faster. Faster vibrations result in higher-pitched sounds.

  - amount of vibrating material. Increasing the amount (thickness) of a string lowers the pitch of a sound. Heavier (thicker) strings have more mass to move, so vibrate more slowly. Slower vibrations result in lower-pitched sounds.

Why sounds become softer the further you are away

- Vibrations send out sound waves in all directions.

- Sound waves spread the energy from the vibrations over a wider area as they travel further from the vibrating source.

- Energy of the vibrations that reach the ear become less. This is why we see cars on a distant motorway, even though we cannot hear them.

Problems caused by loud sounds

- Temporary deafness will occur if the eardrum is perforated by loud bangs. Deafness is temporary because the eardrum is able to repair itself.

- Permanent deafness might occur because of damage done to the inner ear by very loud sounds.

- Loud sounds speed up damage to the ear. This results in reducing the range of frequencies that can be heard.

5.11 A table is a non-luminous source and yet we can see it. Explain how this is possible. (2)

5.12 Write down the words that complete the following sentences:

    (a) Light rays will pass through _____ materials and you can see clear images through them. (1)

    (b) Light rays cannot pass through _____ materials at all. Such materials block light rays and form shadows. (1)

    (c) Some light rays are changed as they pass through _____ materials, which means that you cannot see a clear image of what is on the other side. (1)

5.13 What happens when a light ray hits a mirror and what is this called? (2)

5.14 How are sound waves produced? (2)

5.15 (a) Describe how you would make a guitar string produce a musical note. (2)

    (b) How would you make the note higher? (2)

    (c) How would you make the sound louder? (1)

5.16 Why can we not hear the vast explosions that constantly take place on the Sun? ('The huge distance' is not the answer!) (2)

5.4 Earth and space

The solar system

- The nearest star to the Earth is the Sun.
- The Earth and other main planets orbit the Sun, making what is known as the solar system.
- The Earth, Sun and all the planets are approximately spherical in shape.
- A planet is a body that orbits a star.
- The Earth takes 365¼ days to orbit the Sun – this is called a year.
- The Earth spins on its own axis and makes one complete turn every 24 hours – this is called a day.

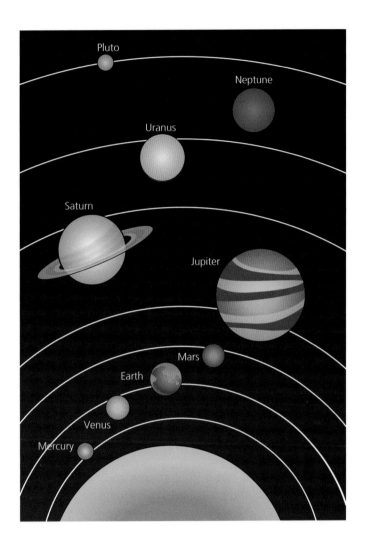

> ### → Revision tip
> To help you remember the order of the main planets, use the phrase:
> **M**y **V**ery **E**ccentric **M**other **J**ust **S**hot **U**ncle **N**orman

- The Earth is one of eight main planets that, along with the dwarf planet Pluto, orbit the Sun.

- As the Earth spins:

  - half of it is lit up by the Sun – daytime

  - the other half is in darkness – night-time.

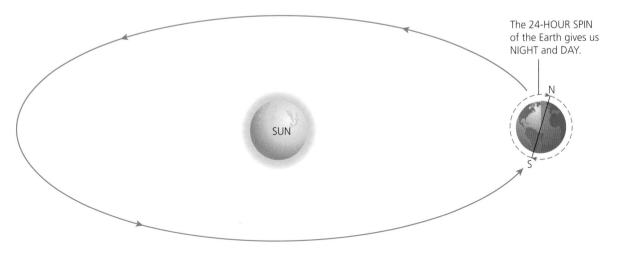

The 24-HOUR SPIN of the Earth gives us NIGHT and DAY.

■ The Sun and the Earth

Sunshine and shadows

- The Sun appears to rise in the east, become high at midday and appears to set in the west. In fact, the Sun does not move, it is the spinning of the Earth that causes this.

- Opaque objects that block out sunlight cause shadows. These vary in length and direction throughout the day.

Time of day	Position of sun	Shadow
Morning	Sun is low in the sky	Shadows are long and point west.
Midday	Sun is high in the sky	Shadows are shortest and point north.
Evening	Sun is low in the sky	Shadows are long and point east.

- The changing length and direction of shadows is used in the design of sundials, which are used to tell the time of day.

The Moon

- A moon is a body that orbits a planet.

- The general name given to a body that orbits a planet is a satellite.

- Each of the planets, except Mercury and Venus, has at least one satellite (called a moon) that orbits them.

- The Earth has one satellite (the Moon) and this orbits the Earth once every 27 days. This period of time is called a lunar month.

- The Moon is not a light source and it is hard to see during daytime. We see it best at night because light from the Sun is reflected from it.

- We do not always see the whole Moon all the time: it appears to change shape at different times of the month. We call these changes in the shape of the Moon phases.

? **Exam-style questions**

Try these questions. The answers are given at the back of the book.

5.17 Why do we experience night and day? (1)

5.18 What causes the Sun to appear to move across the sky? (1)

5.19 Explain the difference in the appearance of shadows cast at midday and in the evening. (2)

5.20 How long is a lunar month and what does this period of time represent? (2)

5.21 Why can we see the Moon better at night than in the daytime? (2)

★ Make sure you know

- ★ The basic elements of an electric circuit.
- ★ How to draw electric circuits and circuit symbols.
- ★ The effect of adding different elements to circuits.
- ★ The main types and features of forces.
- ★ The main features of light.
- ★ The main features of sound.
- ★ The main features of the solar system.

Revision tip

Use the glossary at the back of the book for definitions of key words.

Test yourself ✔

Before moving on to the next chapter, make sure you can answer the following questions. The answers are at the back of the book.

1 Draw and label the following circuit symbols:

   (a) A lamp

   (b) A cell

   (c) A switch

   (d) A motor

2 If lamps and cells are connected in series, what does this mean?

3 What is a force?

4 What do we measure force in?

5 What do we use to measure force?

6 What is gravity?

7 What does gravity never do?

8 Give three examples of luminous sources.

9 Name two important features that describe how light travels.

10 (a) How long does it take for the Earth to complete one orbit of the Sun?

   (b) What do we call this period of time?

11 What is the difference between a moon and a planet?

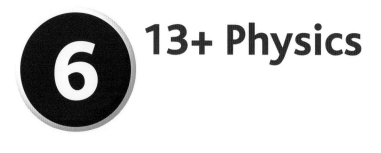

13+ Physics

6.1 Density

Mass

- The mass of something tells us how much matter is present.
- The standard unit of mass is the kilogram (kg), but you will normally measure mass in grams (g).
- There is no verb 'to mass', so we call the activity weighing. Objects are weighed on balances (or scales) and the mass is read off the scale in kilograms or grams.

> **→ Exam tip**
>
> Do not confuse mass and weight:
>
> - Mass is the amount of material in a body – measured in kilograms (or grams).
> - Weight is the downward force exerted by a body because of gravity – measured in newtons (N).

Volume

- Volume tells us how big a solid object is. In the case of a liquid, it tells us how much liquid we have.
- In the laboratory, it is usual to measure volume in cubic centimetres (cm^3).

It is usual to measure the volume of liquids by using a measuring cylinder. Some measuring cylinders are marked in litres (l) or millilitres (ml). As 1 litre of water has almost the same volume as $1000\,cm^3$, it is perfectly satisfactory to measure liquids in cm^3.

Measuring the volume of solids

When measuring regular-shaped solids simply measure the length (l), width (w) and height (h) and multiply them together:

volume = $l \times w \times h$ cm^3

A non-porous solid will push away (displace) water. This is used to measure the volume of an irregular-shaped solid:

volume of object = amount of water displaced

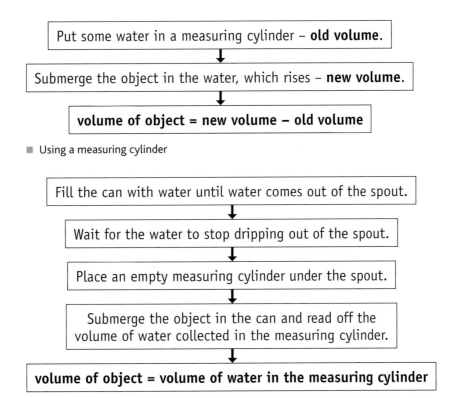

Put some water in a measuring cylinder – **old volume.**

Submerge the object in the water, which rises – **new volume.**

volume of object = new volume – old volume

■ Using a measuring cylinder

Fill the can with water until water comes out of the spout.

Wait for the water to stop dripping out of the spout.

Place an empty measuring cylinder under the spout.

Submerge the object in the can and read off the volume of water collected in the measuring cylinder.

volume of object = volume of water in the measuring cylinder

■ Using a displacement ('Eureka') can

Measuring the volume of gases

Gases fill any container completely, so we measure the size of the container. This could be a measuring cylinder (inverted over water) or, more usually, a gas syringe.

Density

- Each and every substance has its own special number called its **density**, which describes how much matter (mass) is packed into a specified volume (usually $1\,cm^3$) of it.

- Density can be used to identify a substance.

- The density of a material is the mass of each cm^3.

- The unit of density is kg/m^3 or g/cm^3. However, you will usually be working in g/cm^3.

Remembering the unit for density as g/cm^3 will help you to calculate the density of something for the unit tells you that the density of something is its mass divided by its volume.

> **→ Exam tip**
>
> When doing scientific calculations:
>
> - *Never* merely write an answer.
>
> - *Always* show how you arrived at your answer by working stage by stage and writing each stage down.
>
> - *Always* include the unit in your answer – numbers on their own are meaningless.

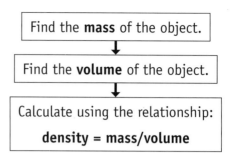

■ Density of solids

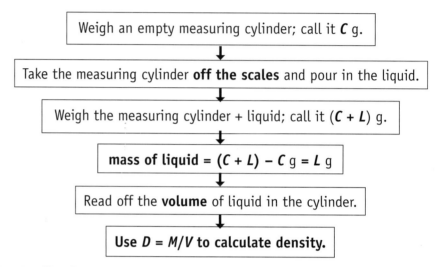

■ Density of liquids

Density of oxygen

Potassium permanganate decomposes when it is heated to form a solid residue and releases oxygen as described by the word equation:

potassium permanganate (s) + heat → residue (s) + oxygen (g)

As total mass at start = total mass at end, then:

mass of oxygen = (mass of potassium permanganate) – (mass of residue)

The **volume** of oxygen is found by collecting the gas in a gas syringe.

Density of carbon dioxide

A similar experiment using the same apparatus can be carried out, this time by heating a suitable carbonate, e.g. copper carbonate instead of potassium permanganate. The experimental procedure is exactly the same; it is the reaction that is different:

copper carbonate (s) + heat → copper oxide (s) + carbon dioxide (g)

? **Exam-style questions**

Try these questions. The answers are given at the back of the book.

6.1 Which two things do you need to know about a substance to be able to find out its density? (2)

6.2 Using the words density, mass and volume, write down the equation that you would use to find density. (3)

6.3 Find the densities of the following blocks of materials:

(a) Material A, mass 750 g, volume 100 cm³. (2)

(b) Material B, mass 220 g, volume 20 cm³. (2)

(c) Material C, mass 540 g, volume 200 cm³. (2)

(d) Material D, mass 162 g, volume 60 cm³. (2)

6.4 In question 6.3, which of the blocks A, B, C, D are made of the same material? Give a reason. (2)

6.5 The density of marble is 3.2 g/cm³; the density of glass is 2.8 g/cm³. If you had 3 kg of each, which material would have the larger volume? (1)

6.6 If the density of air is 1.3×10^{-3} g/cm³, what is the mass of air in a room measuring 10 m × 6 m × 3 m? (2)

6.2 Electricity and electromagnetism

Electricity

- When one end of a conductor has a greater amount of energy than the other, electric charge in the form of electrons will flow in the form of an electric current.

- The energy difference, sometimes called potential (energy) difference or p.d., is measured in volts (V).

- The amount of current is measured in amperes or amps (A) using an ammeter that needs to be connected in series.

- Ammeters must be connected the right way – positive (on ammeter) to positive (on battery/cell).

- A battery is made up of two or more **cells** connected together. A cell or battery transforms **chemical energy** into **electrical energy**, and this electrical energy is changed into other forms in electric components.

Electric circuits

Series circuits

- One path for the current to travel.

- Components are connected one after the other – rather like railway carriages.

- Current is not used up as it goes round a **series circuit**. This means that current is the same at all points in a series circuit.

- Adding more cells, increases the available energy (more volts).

- More components (e.g. lamps, motors) puts more 'things in the way' (increases resistance to the current) so current becomes less.

Parallel circuits

- **Parallel circuits** are two or more individual circuits, each one being connected to the same power supply.

- Each component draws its own supply of current from the cell/battery.

- Adding extra components means more current is drawn so the battery/cell runs down more quickly.

- If one component fails, components in other circuits are not affected.

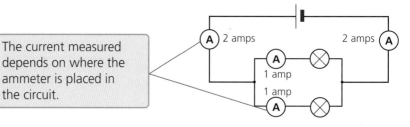

The current measured depends on where the ammeter is placed in the circuit.

2 amps   1 amp   1 amp   2 amps

■ Current in a parallel circuit

■ Fixed-value resistor

Resistance

● **Resistors** transform energy (also known as the heating effect of a current).

● Good conductors (e.g. copper, gold) offer low resistance to current.

● Thick wire offers less resistance to current than thin wire.

Think of a three-lane motorway – traffic flows well – then cones reduce the three lanes to one and traffic flows very slowly as the thin road offers more resistance than the wide motorway. So it is with thick and thin conductors.

Resistors are components designed to reduce current.

The amount of resistance can be measured and is recorded in **ohms** (Ω).

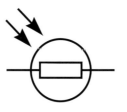

■ Symbols for a variable resistor

Variable resistors are sometimes called 'dimmers'.

■ LDR (light-dependent resistor)

When light falls on a **light-dependent resistor**, the value of its resistance falls. In the dark, an LDR has high resistance.

> **Revision tip**
> Think of **LLL** – An LDR has **L**ow resistance in **L**ight.

Fuses

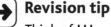

■ Fuse

A fuse is used as a safety device to protect components from damage caused by high currents.

When there is a current in a circuit that is too high for the fuse, the fuse wire heats – melts – and breaks the circuit, stopping all current in the circuit immediately.

Switches

Their function is to complete or break circuits.

● Switch closed: 'ON' – circuit complete; current flows.

● Switch open: 'OFF' – circuit broken; no current flows.

Types of switches include:

● 'normal' toggle switch, e.g. light switch

■ Switch (open)

● push switch, e.g. bell push, mobile phone and computer keys

■ Push-button switch

● reed switch: contacts normally open – needs a magnet to close them.

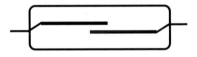

■ Reed switch

Switches in series form a simple 'AND' circuit:

● Used for safety devices in machines, e.g. washing machine doors.

● The motor works only when switches A *and* B are closed.

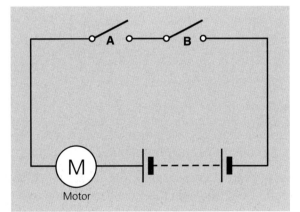

AND circuit: Both switch A **AND** switch B must be on before the motor will run.

● Results can be summarised in a truth table.

● The input is provided by switches A and B.

● The output, in this case, is the motor.

Inputs		Output
Switch A	Switch B	Motor
Off	Off	Off
Off	On	Off
On	Off	Off
On	On	On

- Switch ON: current flows – represented by 1.
- Switch OFF: no current – represented by 0.
- Output is represented by Q.

Inputs		Output
A	B	Q
0	0	0
0	1	0
1	0	0
1	1	1

Switches in parallel form a simple 'OR' circuit:

- Used for burglar alarms, car interior lights.
- The bell sounds when switches A OR B, OR BOTH, are closed.

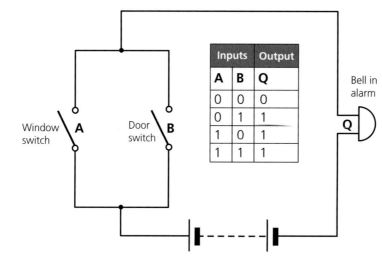

Inputs		Output
A	B	Q
0	0	0
0	1	1
1	0	1
1	1	1

Window switch A   Door switch B   Bell in alarm

OR circuit: If either switch A or switch B is on the alarm will sound.

Diodes

- Made from materials called semiconductors, which allow current to flow through them one way, but almost no current to flow through the other.
- Used to protect components that would be damaged if current flowed through them the wrong way, e.g. in radios and computers.
- Their purpose is to allow current to flow in one direction only.
- Current flows in the same direction in which the arrow on the symbol points.

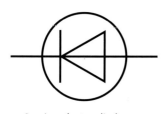

■ Semiconductor diode

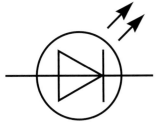

- A **light-emitting diode** emits light when a small current flows through it.
- A protective resistor is always connected in series with an LED to protect it from damage caused by too large a current flowing through it.
- Must be connected the right way.

■ Light-emitting diode

Magnetism

See Chapter 5, Section 5.2 for details of:

- magnetic **poles**
- how magnets behave.

Testing magnets

- Magnets will settle and point to magnetic north when freely suspended.
- Magnets will attract only other magnetic materials, e.g. iron (steel).
- Magnets will be repulsed by another magnet – this is the only true test to identify a magnet.

Magnetic field

- The area around a magnet where a magnetic force can be detected.

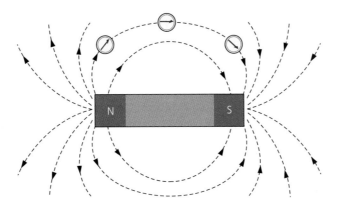

- The lines are called lines of force.
- The arrows show the direction in which the force acts.

> **→ Revision tip**
> The direction of the force can be remembered by the word 'NAST':
> **N**orth **A**way – **S**outh **T**owards.

- The spacing of the lines tells us the strength of the field. Lines closer together show a stronger field than lines further apart.
- The lines are invisible – we only see them because of the use of iron filings.

Using electricity to make magnets – the magnetic effect of an electric current

Making an electromagnet

- When an electric current flows through a wire, a magnetic field around the wire is produced.

- A compass needle shows that this magnetic field has direction.

- If the direction of the current is changed, the needle points in the opposite direction.

- If the wire is formed into a loop, the magnetic field will be in one direction, at right angles to the loop.

- If more loops are added using insulated wire, as in a coil, there is a strong magnetic field inside the coil that:

  - ceases if the current stops flowing

  - is in one particular direction

  - will reverse in direction if the direction of the current is reversed.

- A soft iron rod (core) placed inside the coil will become a magnet when the current is switched on.

To make an electromagnet stronger:

- add more turns of insulated wire to the coil

- increase the current

- add a 'core' of soft iron.

Using an electromagnet

Metal scrapyards:

- Iron and steel can be separated from non-magnetic materials.

- Iron can be lifted, moved and dropped where it is needed when the current is switched off.

Relays:

- A relay is a switch that is operated by an electromagnet and consists of two separate circuits:

  - Circuit 1: the ON/OFF switch controls a small current that is used to make a coil into a magnet. The magnet operates the relay to close the switch in circuit 2.

  - Circuit 2: the 'end use' circuit (e.g. car starter motor) – currents in these circuits can be quite large.

> **?** Exam-style questions
>
> Try these questions. The answers are given at the back of the book.
>
> 6.7 (a) Draw a circuit that contains two cells, a lamp and an ammeter in series. (4)
>
> (b) What happens to the ammeter reading if another lamp is added to the circuit? (1)
>
> (c) What must you be careful about when connecting the ammeter? (1)

6.8   Look at the circuit below:

(a) Which switch:

  (i)   controls all lamps?

  (ii) controls lamp 1?   (2)

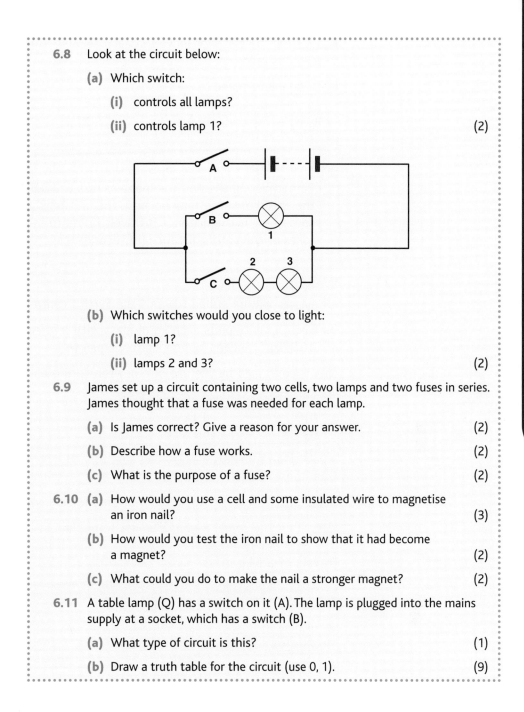

(b) Which switches would you close to light:

  (i)   lamp 1?

  (ii) lamps 2 and 3?   (2)

6.9   James set up a circuit containing two cells, two lamps and two fuses in series. James thought that a fuse was needed for each lamp.

(a) Is James correct? Give a reason for your answer.   (2)

(b) Describe how a fuse works.   (2)

(c) What is the purpose of a fuse?   (2)

6.10 (a) How would you use a cell and some insulated wire to magnetise an iron nail?   (3)

(b) How would you test the iron nail to show that it had become a magnet?   (2)

(c) What could you do to make the nail a stronger magnet?   (2)

6.11 A table lamp (Q) has a switch on it (A). The lamp is plugged into the mains supply at a socket, which has a switch (B).

(a) What type of circuit is this?   (1)

(b) Draw a truth table for the circuit (use 0, 1).   (9)

6.3 Forces and motion, rotation and pressure

See also Chapter 5, Section 5.2 for:

● what a force is

● what a force can do.

Speed

● This is a measure of how fast something is moving.

● We need to measure:

  • the distance the object moves (in m)

  • the time it takes to move this distance (in s).

- Speed is the distance moved in each second. This gives us the unit of speed as m/s.

- To calculate speed:

$$\text{speed} = \frac{\text{distance}}{\text{time}} \quad \left(\text{or } S = \frac{D}{T}\right)$$

Exam tip

Remembering the unit for speed as m/s will help you to calculate the speed of something because the unit tells you that the speed of something is the distance it travels (in metres – m) divided by the time it takes to travel this distance (in seconds – s).

Weight

All masses will be pulled towards the Earth's centre by gravitational force (g).

On Earth, gravity pulls each kg of mass with a force of about 10 N, i.e. we say g ≈ 10 N/kg (≈ means 'approximately equal to').

This is confirmed by the use of a newton spring balance (or newton meter).

Mass	Weight (reading on newton meter)
1 kg	10 N
2 kg	20 N
0.5 kg	5 N

From these results, we can see that:

weight (N) = mass (kg) × gravitational force (N/kg)

Mass stays the *same*; *weight changes* from planet to planet.

Travels of a 5 kg mass

Earth	Earth's Moon	Outer space
mass = 5 kg	mass = 5 kg	mass = 5 kg
g = 10 N/kg	g = 1.6 N/kg	g = 0
weight = 5 kg × 10 N/kg	weight = 5 kg × 1.6 N/kg	weight = 5 kg × 0 N/kg
= 50 N	= 8 N	= 0*

*This is why masses become weightless in space.

Balanced forces

- Forces are always in pairs in opposite directions.

- When the forces are equal, the forces are balanced – no movement (if object is stationary) or change in movement (if object is moving) happens.

- If one force is bigger than the other, the forces are unbalanced – movement happens in the direction in which the larger force acts.

NO MOVEMENT

MOVEMENT TO THE RIGHT

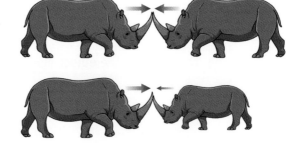

Stationary objects

- The downward force exerted by the weight of a book at rest on a table, is balanced by the upward force exerted by the table.

- A boat floats because the downward force exerted by the weight of the boat is balanced by the upward force (upthrust) exerted by the water.

Moving objects

- If a force acts on a moving body in the same direction as the movement, the body will increase in speed (i.e. accelerate). For example:

  - Gravity increases the speed of falling objects.

  - Pedalling harder makes your bicycle go faster.

- If a force acts on a moving body in the opposite direction from the movement, then the body will decrease in speed (i.e. slow down).

- When the two opposing forces are equal (i.e. are balanced), the body will move at a constant speed.

- When the two opposing forces are not equal (i.e. are unbalanced), the body will change speed and/or direction.

Friction – the force that opposes motion

- Objects moving through the air will rub against air particles that slow them down. This is a form of friction called air resistance (drag).

- To reduce the effect of air resistance, bodies are given pointed fronts, sleek designs and smooth surfaces, i.e. they are streamlined.

- When two surfaces rub together, the force of friction:

  - opposes the motion. For example, after they have opened their parachutes, parachutists slow down as they fall, until the upward force of air resistance is balanced by their weight and they then fall at a constant speed.

  - releases energy in the form of heat. For example, brake pads on cars and bicycles become hot as the force of friction between them and the moving wheel releases heat; people camping might rub two sticks together to generate enough heat to light a fire.

Changing shape – elastic bodies

Bodies that are able to change shape when a force is exerted on them, and return to their original shape when the force is removed, are said to be **elastic**.

Changing shapes of springs

This usually involves measuring the extension of the spring when increasing force is applied.

extension = new length – original length

The extension is in proportion to the loads applied and the spring returns to its original length when the force is removed – it is elastic.

This feature of springs is why they are used in the construction of newton meters.

The spring is elastic until a load is added, which causes the spring not to return to its original length. The extension is now not in direct proportion to the load applied and the elastic limit of the spring has been exceeded.

Extensive work on elastic bodies was carried out by Robert Hooke who was able to give us a law about the stretching of elastic bodies such as springs.

Hooke's law states that when a force is applied to a spring, it will extend in direct proportion to the force applied and go back to its original length, provided that the elastic limit is not exceeded.

Extensions of combinations of similar springs

Springs in series:

total extension = extension of one spring × number of springs

Springs in parallel ('sharing the load – side by side'):

$$\text{total extension} = \frac{\text{extension of one spring}}{\text{number of springs}}$$

Turning forces – levers

● A lever is any rigid body that is able to turn about a pivot.

● Forces that cause levers to turn are called turning moments.

turning moment (Nm) = size of force (N) × distance from pivot (m)

Balancing levers

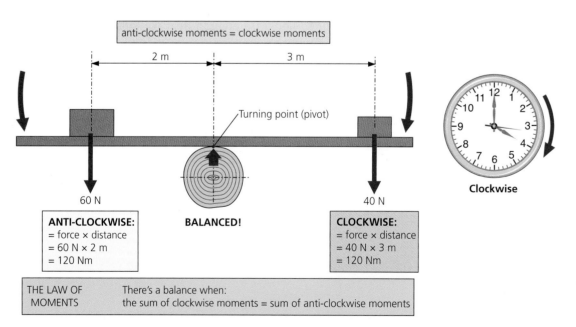

anti-clockwise moments = clockwise moments

2 m | 3 m

Turning point (pivot)

60 N | 40 N

Clockwise

ANTI-CLOCKWISE:
= force × distance
= 60 N × 2 m
= 120 Nm

BALANCED!

CLOCKWISE:
= force × distance
= 40 N × 3 m
= 120 Nm

THE LAW OF MOMENTS — There's a balance when: the sum of clockwise moments = sum of anti-clockwise moments

The **principle of moments** means that there is a balance when:

● sum of clockwise moments = sum of anti-clockwise moments

● a smaller force is able to balance a larger force

● the smaller force is further away from the pivot than the larger force.

This is why:

● it is easier to dig soil with a long-handled spade rather than a short-handled trowel

● door handles are placed as far away from the hinges (**pivot**) as possible

● long door handles are easier to turn than door knobs.

Combining levers

● Scissors, pliers and wire cutters all involve two levers that turn about the same pivot.

● The force you exert is called the effort and the force exerted, i.e. that does the cutting, is called the load.

● Cutting tools always have longer handles than blades. For example:

  • garden shears for cutting hedges have longer handles than scissors used for cutting paper

  • tin snips used to cut metal sheets have longer handles than electrical wire cutters.

Pulleys and gears — other types of machine

● A pulley is a wheel that can change the direction of a force. A combination of pulleys enables a small force to move a larger force.

● A gear is a wheel with grooves cut into its circumference. These grooves are called teeth. If such a gear wheel is turned by a motor and its teeth are interlocked with the teeth of a smaller gearwheel with fewer teeth, then the smaller wheel will turn faster than the motor wheel. Using gears helps cyclists to peddle uphill easier or increase speed when going downhill.

Pressure

The force acting on each m² is known as pressure.

To calculate the pressure exerted by one surface on another, we use the relationship:

$$\text{pressure} = \frac{\text{force applied}}{\text{area}} \left(P = \frac{F}{A} \right)$$

The unit of pressure is N/m².

1 N/m² is also called 1 pascal (Pa).

Remembering the unit for pressure as N/m² will help you to calculate the amount of pressure being exerted, for the unit tells you that pressure is the force being applied (in newtons – N) divided by the area over which the force acts (in square metres – m²).

Pressure in action

Decreasing the area over which a force acts increases the pressure. For example:

● sports shoes – studs/spikes

● any sharp point or blade.

Increasing the area over which a force acts decreases the pressure. For example:

- tank/bulldozer caterpillar tracks
- skis, snow-shoes.

Try these questions. The answers are given at the back of the book.

6.12 On Earth, gravity exerts a force of 10 N/kg. Calculate the weight of the following masses:

    (a) 3 kg   (2)

    (b) 30 kg   (2)

    (c) 180 kg   (2)

    (d) 500 g   (2)

    (e) 320 g   (2)

6.13 On Earth, gravity exerts a force of 10 N/kg and the Moon exerts a force of 1.6 N/kg. An astronaut has a mass of 40 kg on Earth.

    (a) What is his mass on the Moon?   (2)

    (b) What is his weight on Earth?   (2)

    (c) What is his weight on the Moon?   (2)

6.14 Write down the word or words that best complete each of the following sentences.

    (a) If a force acts on a moving body in the same direction as the movement, then the body will _____ in speed (i.e. _____).   (2)

    (b) If a force acts on a moving body in the opposite direction from the movement, then the body will _____ in speed.   (1)

    (c) When the two opposing forces are equal (i.e. are balanced), the body will move at a _____.   (1)

6.15 You have seven springs that are all similar. You test one of them and find that it extends 8 cm when a load of 100 g is applied.

    (a) What would be the total extension if you connect three of them together in series and put on a load of 200 g?   (2)

    (b) What would be the total extension if you connect four of them together in parallel and put on a load of 200 g?   (2)

6.16 A man turns a nut by exerting a force of 300 N at the end of a spanner that is 15 cm long. What is the turning moment applied to the nut?   (2)

6.17 If a turning moment of 8 Nm were produced at a point 0.8 m from the hinge of a door, what force was used to achieve this?   (2)

6.18 A boy of mass 40 kg sits 270 cm from the centre of a see-saw. A girl of mass 30 kg sits on the other side. Where must she sit to enable the see-saw to balance?   (2)

6.19 A box has a weight of 60 N. Write down what pressure it will exert on the ground if the area of the base is:

    (a) 10 cm²   (2)

    (b) 12 cm²   (2)

    (c) 0.06 cm²   (2)

6.20 A block weighs 100 N and exerts a pressure of 25 N/cm² when placed on a table. What is the area of the box in contact with the table?   (2)

6.4 Waves including light waves and sound waves

Light

We see objects because light energy activates the receptors found in the **retina** of our eyes

The light entering our eyes can come from two sources.

Luminous sources

Some objects, for instance the Sun, a table lamp and a television set, give out their own light in the form of light waves.

Reflection from non-luminous objects

Most things, for example a book a table or the Moon, do not give out their own light, but we can see them because light from a luminous source is reflected into our eyes.

Features of light rays

- They are very fast – at present nothing is known to travel faster and their speed through a vacuum is 300 000 000 m/s (usually written as 3.0×10^8 m/s).
- They travel in straight lines – you cannot see round corners.
- When they travel through materials without being absorbed, such materials are called transparent.
- They will not travel through opaque materials – shadows are formed.
- They can be absorbed (important when looking at the colour of objects) and re-emitted in all directions in a process called scattering, by materials that are said to be translucent.

Reflection of light

- When light rays hit a surface, they may bounce off it – this is reflection.
- Smooth surfaces (e.g. mirrors) reflect all of the light in one direction.
- Rough surfaces (e.g. paper) reflect the light in many directions – the light has been scattered.

How plane mirrors reflect light

- A plane mirror is one that is flat.
- The **normal** is an imaginary line at 90° to the surface of the mirror that is used for measuring angles.
- Rays coming from a light source to the mirror are called **incident rays** and they hit the mirror at the **angle of incidence**.

- Rays bouncing away from the mirror are called **reflected rays** and they move away at the angle of reflection.

angle of incidence = angle of reflection

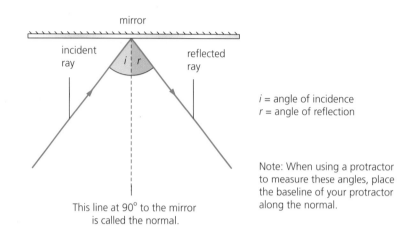

i = angle of incidence
r = angle of reflection

Note: When using a protractor to measure these angles, place the baseline of your protractor along the normal.

This line at 90° to the mirror is called the normal.

Using mirrors

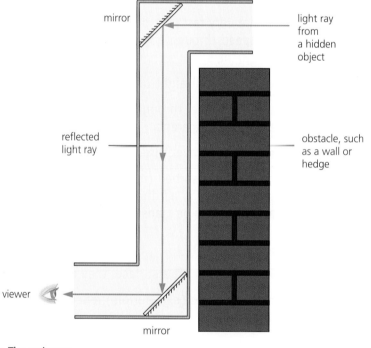

mirror

light ray from a hidden object

reflected light ray

obstacle, such as a wall or hedge

viewer

mirror

■ The periscope

Refraction of light

Light will travel at different speeds, depending on what it is travelling through. For example:

Medium travelling through	Speed of light
Air	3.0×10^8 m/s
Water	2.25×10^8 m/s
Glass	2.0×10^8 m/s

- When light travels from air into water, it slows down and bends towards the normal.

- When light travels from water into air, it speeds up and bends away from the normal.

- The bending of light as it reaches the boundary between different materials is called **refraction**.

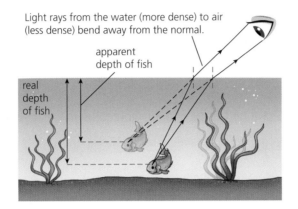

Light rays from the water (more dense) to air (less dense) bend away from the normal.

apparent depth of fish

real depth of fish

Colour

Sir Isaac Newton shone a beam of white light through a prism and found that it split up into all the colours of the rainbow, with the colours in the following order:

red – orange – yellow – green – blue – indigo – violet

To help you remember the order of the colours, use the phrase: **R**ichard **O**f **Y**ork **G**ave **B**attle **I**n **V**ain.

- The display on a screen resulting from the splitting of white light into its colours is called a **spectrum**.

- In the case of white light, the colours run into each other, forming a continuous spectrum – such as you can see in a rainbow.

- The splitting of white light into its colours is called **dispersion**.

- Raindrops act as little prisms and disperse white sunlight into the colours that we see as a rainbow.

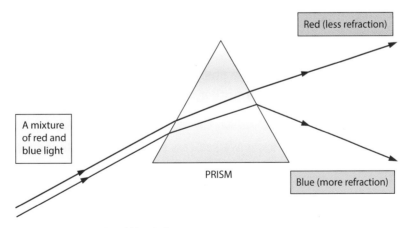

Red (less refraction)

A mixture of red and blue light

PRISM

Blue (more refraction)

■ Refraction of red and blue light

Sound

- If you clamp a hacksaw blade at one end, pull up and release the other end it will move up and down in a series of vibrations.
- Vibrations are carried through the air as sound waves.
- Sound waves are made up of sequences of squashing–stretching–squashing... and so on.
  - As the blade moves down it squashes the air below – squashing.
  - As the blade moves up it stretches the air below – stretching
- Sound waves need 'something' to squash and stretch, so can only travel through substances that contain atoms and/or molecules.
- There are no atoms and/or molecules in a vacuum.
- Therefore sound waves cannot travel through a vacuum.

Speed of sound waves

The speed of sound waves depends upon the material (medium) through which they travel.

Medium	Speed (in m/s)
Gases (air)	330
Liquids (water)	1500
Solids (metal)	5000

Sound waves travel much slower than light waves.

Medium (air)	Speed (in m/s)
Light waves	300 000 000
Sound waves	330

- Light waves are a million times faster than sound waves.
- This is why we see lightning before we hear the thunderclap.

Loudness of sound

- The size of the vibration is called its amplitude.
- The greater the amplitude, the louder the sound.

Why sounds become softer the further you are away

- Vibrations send out sound waves in all directions.
- Sound waves spread the energy from the vibrations over a wider area as they travel further from the vibrating source.
- Energy of the vibrations that reach the ear becomes less.
- This is why we see cars on a distant motorway, even though we cannot hear them.

Pitch of sound

- The number of complete vibrations in a specified time (cycles per second) is called the frequency.
- A faster vibration (i.e. higher frequency) produces a sound that has a higher note, or more correctly a note of a higher pitch.

A high frequency of vibration results in a note of high pitch. A low frequency of vibration results in a note of low pitch.

- Frequency is measured in Hertz (Hz).

- Frequencies audible to the human ear are in the range of 20–20 000 Hz.

- Bats are able to hear sounds of frequency of over 100 000 Hz – these sounds are inaudible to the human ear.

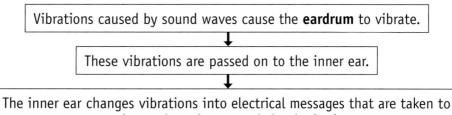

> Vibrations caused by sound waves cause the **eardrum** to vibrate.
>
> ↓
>
> These vibrations are passed on to the inner ear.
>
> ↓
>
> The inner ear changes vibrations into electrical messages that are taken to and sorted out into sounds by the **brain**.

■ How we hear

Problems caused by loud sounds

- Temporary deafness will occur if the eardrum is perforated by loud bangs. Deafness is temporary because the eardrum is able to repair itself.

- Permanent deafness might occur because of damage done to the inner ear by very loud sounds.

- Loud sounds speed up damage to the ear. This reduces the range of frequencies that can be heard.

? **Exam-style questions**

Try these questions. The answers are given at the back of the book.

6.21 Light rays are emitted from a luminous source. List three other facts about light rays. (3)

6.22 (a) What is refraction? (1)

    (b) Where does this happen? (1)

    (c) Why does this happen? (1)

6.23 (a) Using two mirrors, design an instrument for looking over a high wall. (4)

    (b) What is the name of your instrument? (1)

6.24 The speed of sound in air is about 300 m/s. If thunder is heard 10 seconds after the lightning is seen, how far away is the storm? (2)

6.25 A man fires a gun and hears the echo from a building 550 m away. If the speed of sound in air is 330 m/s, how long after firing the gun will he hear the echo? (2)

6.26 (a) What feature of a sound wave determines the (i) pitch, (ii) loudness, of a note? (2)

    (b) Use the features you have described in (a) to describe two differences between a high, loud note and a low, quiet one. (2)

See Chapter 5, Section 5.4 for the Earth's place in the solar system and how we experience day and night.

Reasons for the seasons

The Earth's axis is not vertical, but is tilted by about 23°. This means that at any one time, part of the Earth's surface is closer to the Sun than at other times, giving us seasons.

Season	Height of sun	Temperature of Earth's surface	Length of shadow	Length of day
Summer	High	Warm	Short	Long
Winter	Low	Cold	Long	Short

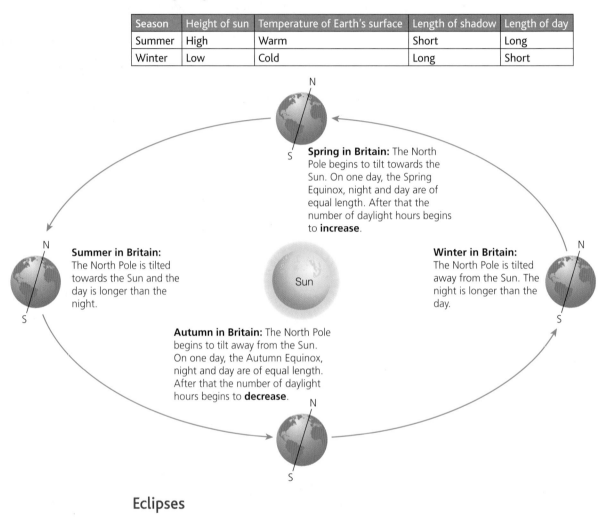

Spring in Britain: The North Pole begins to tilt towards the Sun. On one day, the Spring Equinox, night and day are of equal length. After that the number of daylight hours begins to **increase**.

Summer in Britain: The North Pole is tilted towards the Sun and the day is longer than the night.

Winter in Britain: The North Pole is tilted away from the Sun. The night is longer than the day.

Autumn in Britain: The North Pole begins to tilt away from the Sun. On one day, the Autumn Equinox, night and day are of equal length. After that the number of daylight hours begins to **decrease**.

Eclipses

Eclipse of the Moon (lunar eclipse)

This happens when the Earth is between the Moon and the Sun.

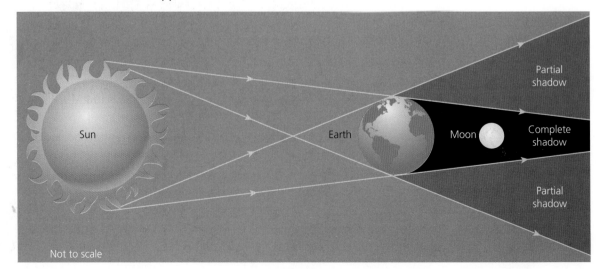

Partial shadow

Complete shadow

Partial shadow

Sun

Earth

Moon

Not to scale

Eclipse of the Sun (solar eclipse)

This happens when the Moon is between the Earth and the Sun.

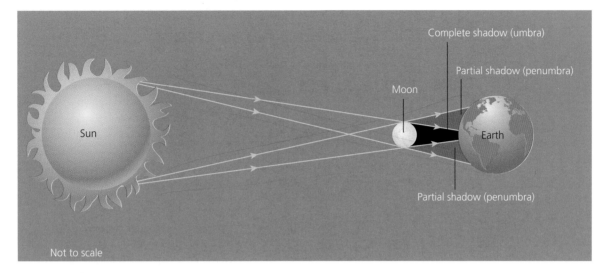

Our place in the universe

- Within the universe there are more than 100 billion galaxies.

- A galaxy is the name given to a group of stars. A galaxy contains over 100 000 stars. Our galaxy (called the Milky Way) is estimated to contain 100 billion.

- The Milky Way is so huge, it takes light 100 000 years to cross it.

- We say that the distance across the Milky Way is 100 000 light years.

- A light year is the distance that light (travelling at 3×10^5 km/s) travels in one year. (It comes to 9×10^{12} km or about 60 000 times greater than the distance from the Earth to the Sun.)

- Our nearest star (called Alpha Centauri) is about 4.2 light years away.

- We can see stars because they are luminous sources and give out light.

- We see planets because they reflect light from the Sun.

- The planets in our solar system are held in their orbits by gravitational attraction between them and the Sun.

Satellites

A satellite is something that orbits a larger body in the solar system. Their forward motion and gravitational force keeps them in orbit.

Natural satellites include:

- planets orbiting the Sun

- the Moon orbiting the Earth.

Artificial satellites are man-made and are launched into space for a particular purpose. For example:

- observation of the Earth for weather forecasting; geological surveys

- observation for military purposes

- communications: satellite TV, radio, mobile phones

- observing space, e.g. Hubble telescope.

> **?** **Exam-style questions**
> Try these questions. The answers are given at the back of the book.
>
> 6.27 What causes us to have seasons on Earth? (2)
>
> 6.28 Write the words that complete the following sentences:
>
> (a) An eclipse of the Moon (lunar eclipse) happens when the _____ is between the Moon and the _____. (2)
>
> (b) An eclipse of the Sun (solar eclipse) happens when the _____ is between the _____ and the Sun. (2)
>
> 6.29 What does the term *light year* refer to? (1)
>
> 6.30 The Hubble telescope operates from a satellite. Why should this provide better pictures of space than land-based telescopes? (2)

6.6 Energy resources, changes in systems and conservation of energy

Work and energy

- Energy is work that has been done *or* work that is able to be done.
- If anything happens, then energy has been supplied.
- For anything to happen, a supply of energy is needed.

What is 'anything'?

Another description could be 'job'. Examples of jobs include:

- an animal moving, eating, living
- a kettle heating water
- a battery of cells making a radio produce sound.

The size of the job (called work) can be measured and the unit of work is called the **joule** (J).

As we cannot measure energy as such, we measure the amount of work done. Work is done when:

- a force produces motion
- something is heated.

Clearly, more work will have been done if:

- you run 200 m instead of 50 m
- you boil 2000 cm³ of cold water rather than 250 cm³.

amount of work done (J) = amount of energy supplied (J)

So the unit we use to measure energy is the joule (1000 J = 1 kJ).

Forms of energy

Kinetic energy (KE)

● This is energy that a body has because it is *moving*.

● The amount of kinetic energy that a body has depends upon two factors:

  • the mass (m) of the moving object

  • the speed (v) of the moving body.

Potential energy (PE)

● This is energy that a body has because of its position or condition.

● PE is a measure of work that is *able to be done*.

Gravitational potential energy (GPE)

● A 'bomb' jump from a diving board will make a bigger splash if done from a higher board.

● A large adult will make a bigger splash when doing the same jump than a smaller youth.

● In both cases, the jumpers fall because gravity pulls their masses downwards towards the Earth's centre.

The amount of **gravitational potential energy** that a body has depends upon three factors:

● the mass (m) of the body

● the vertical height (h) through which the body falls – or can fall

● the force of gravity (g) acting on the body.

Elastic potential energy (strain energy)

● Winding up a clockwork toy; the more turns you make, the further/faster the toy will move.

● The number of turns is a measure of the **strain** put on the spring.

● Pulling back the string of a bow to shoot an arrow; the further you pull back the string (from its normal 'resting' position), the more the bow is under strain and the further the arrow will fly as the bow returns to its original shape.

● More and more energy is stored in the bow as it bends and changes shape.

Chemical energy

● When chemicals react, they change and form new substances.

● During chemical change, energy is released. For example:

  • Burning magnesium will change chemical energy into radiation energy (heat and light).

  • The chemicals of an electric cell will, when a circuit is complete, change chemical energy into electrical energy.

Electrical energy

- Electric currents move energy from one place to another.

- When things move, work is done and so energy has been used.

- This energy is used to make other things happen. For example:

  - a lamp shining

  - a motor turning.

Thermal energy (heat)

- All matter consists of molecules that are constantly in motion (i.e. have KE).

- If you add together the KE of all the molecules, the sum is called the **internal energy** of the substance.

- Adding energy (heating) increases the KE of the molecules, so the internal energy rises.

- The rise in internal energy can be detected by a rise in temperature.

So, the form of energy that brings about a rise in internal energy and, hence, temperature of a substance, is known as **thermal energy** (sometimes this has also been known as heat energy).

During heating and cooling:

- Thermal energy tends to flow from a warm place to a colder one.

- Bodies that absorb energy, become warmer.

- Bodies that emit (lose) energy, become cooler.

Sound energy

Vibrating bodies will give out energy in the form of sound waves that are able to travel through solids, liquids and gases, but not through a vacuum (see Section 6.4).

Light energy

Energy from the Sun is carried by waves. The many types of electromagnetic wave include light waves.

- Light waves enable us to see objects (see Section 6.4).

- Light waves are absorbed by plants and provide the energy for the chemical reactions that change water and carbon dioxide into sugar and oxygen (photosynthesis).

Changing energy from one form to another

- When we say that we are using energy, we are really changing energy from one form to another.

- Energy is never used up, it changes from one form to another.

- The process of changing energy from one form to another is called transferring energy.

- A component is anything that will change energy from one form to another.

- We can list the transferring of energy from one form to another in an energy chain.

- In an energy chain listing energy transfers, along with other forms, heat is always released.

Form of energy at start	Component	Form/s of energy at end
Electrical	Lamp	Light, heat
Chemical	Cell	Electrical, heat
Chemical	Bunsen burner	Light, sound, heat
Sound	Microphone	Electrical, heat
Electrical	Loudspeaker	Sound, heat
Electrical	Motor	Kinetic, sound, heat
Kinetic	Dynamo/generator	Electrical, sound, heat
Light	Solar/cell	Electrical, heat

Law of conservation of energy

When energy changes form:

total amount of energy at the start = total amount of energy at the end

There are *no* exceptions to this law.

Energy cannot be used twice

- A lamp changes electrical energy into heat and light.

- Light is 'useful'; heat is 'wasted' – both are radiated out into space and cannot be used again.

- If 10J of energy are used to light a lamp, we will not obtain 10J worth of light, as much of the energy will be 'wasted' in the form of heat as the lamp warms.

Where does energy come from?

The Sun is a renewable source of energy, as energy from the Sun will be radiated for the foreseeable future. A renewable source is one that can be replenished within a lifetime.

Most of the Earth's energy comes from the Sun. For example:

- Direct heat rays from the Sun can be collected and focused in one place, as in a solar furnace.

- Radiation from the Sun can be changed into electrical energy by a solar cell.

- Plants use radiation from the Sun as the supply of energy for photosynthesis, which changes carbon dioxide and water into oxygen and sugars and starch, which increases biomass and is a supply of chemical energy. This supply of chemical energy can be used as a source of food – changed into thermal energy as animals respire and do work. It can also be used in the production of fuel, for example:

  - wood: an important fuel

  - production of methane: from rotting vegetation

  - production of alcohol: from sugar plants that are allowed to ferment.

Radiation from the Sun causes some parts of the Earth to become hotter than others.

↓

This results in **convection currents** being set up in oceans and the atmosphere.

↓

These currents drive the winds and waves, changing the Sun's radiated energy into **kinetic energy. This is also called wind/wave energy.**

Radiation from the Sun causes water to evaporate from oceans and lakes.

↓

The evaporated water rises, is carried by winds and may fall as rain on high ground. Now the water has **gravitational potential energy**.

↓

As the water falls back to the sea, its gravitational potential energy is changed to **kinetic energy** which enables the water to: – Wear away the mountainside: erosion. – Turn a water wheel: e.g. a flour mill. – Turn a turbine: hydroelectricity. This is also called **falling water energy.**

The Sun is also the initial supply of energy for the fossil fuels, which are non-renewable sources of energy.

Generation of electricity

Electricity may be generated using renewable or non-renewable resources.

Renewable resources

- Renewable resources are either constantly available or can be replaced rapidly.
- They cause little or no atmospheric pollution.
- They are often expensive to exploit.
- They may not be reliable, e.g. wind energy, wave energy, solar energy.

Hydroelectric power:

- Water rushes at great speed past turbine blades, which turn, causing the rotor to turn.

Wind power:

- The blades of a wind turbine are giant propellers that are located high in the air to catch as much wind as possible.
- Many wind turbines are located together in what are called 'wind farms'.

Geothermal power:

- The temperature of the Earth's centre is about 6000°C.
- Electricity can be generated from hot water or steam from the hot interior of the Earth.

Solar power:

- Light energy from the Sun can be changed into electricity by solar cells.

- Each cell produces a small amount of electricity, so a large number of these is required to make a useful amount.

- The effectiveness of these relies on a plentiful supply of sunlight.

Tidal power:

- Rotation of the Earth, together with gravitational forces between the Earth and Moon, cause the water of the oceans to be pulled into 'heaps', resulting in high tides about twice a day.

- Water that is trapped at high tide has gravitational potential energy and this can be changed to kinetic energy and used to drive turbines.

Wave power:

- The constant up and down movement of a sea wave can be changed into rotary motion, which is used to turn a rotor to generate electricity.

Nuclear power:

- Energy is produced when the nuclei of atoms are changed, for example when atoms are split.

Biomass:

- Heat is created by burning wood or other plant material.

Non-renewable resources (fossil fuels)

- Fossil fuels do not become useful until the stored energy within them is released by combining them with oxygen when they burn.

- Once fossil fuels have burned, they cannot be replaced.

- Fossil fuels are also used as raw materials in the manufacture of many substances (plastics, medicines, cosmetics). A world without oil does not merely affect the motor car!

- It has taken over 100 million years to form coal, gas and oil and it is likely that we will have taken a few hundred years to use up supplies of these.

- Burning fossil fuels releases polluting gases such as carbon dioxide and sulfur dioxide into the atmosphere.

- Electricity can be produced more reliably and cheaply in fossil fuel-burning power stations than by using renewable resources.

Thermal power:

- When a coil (rotor) turns inside a magnet (stator), a current of electricity is produced.

- The coil (rotor) is located on the same revolving axle as a set of turbines.

- Steam at high pressure turns the turbine and rotor.

- In order to change water into steam, water can be heated using coal, oil, gas or uranium (in a nuclear reactor).

Coal:

- Millions of years ago plants absorbed energy from the Sun and, through photosynthesis, 'stored' this energy in the form of sugars and starch.

- As plants died and fell into the swamps, the chemical energy stayed 'locked' within them.

- Over a period of at least 100 million years, sediments were laid on top of the plant remains. Pressure increased as more layers were laid on top and the plants hardened and became rock-like (fossils), changing into coal.

Oil and gas:

- Formed millions of years ago from small plants and animals living in the oceans.

- When they died, they sank to the ocean bed and were covered with layers of mud and sediments.

- Over the following millions of years, the decomposed plants and animals changed into oil and gas.

? Exam-style questions

Try these questions. The answers are given at the back of the book.

6.31 (a) What does the word *work* mean? (1)

    (b) What is the unit used to measure energy (1)

    (c) What is the relationship between work and energy? (2)

6.32 What does the law of conservation of energy state? (2)

6.33 Complete the table below. (11)

Form of energy at start	Component	Form/s of energy at end
Electrical	_____	Light, _____
_____	Cell	Electrical, heat
Chemical	Bunsen burner	_____, _____, _____
Sound	Microphone	_____, heat
_____	Loudspeaker	Sound, heat
Electrical	Motor	_____, sound, heat
_____	Dynamo/generator	Electrical, sound, heat
Light	_____	Electrical, heat

6.34 (a) What does the term 'fossil fuel' mean? (2)

    (b) Name two fossil fuels. (2)

    (c) Why are fossil fuels called non-renewable? (2)

    (d) Is burning the only use of fossil fuels? (2)

6.35 It is possible to buy household electric lamps that are said to be more efficient than 'normal' ones.

    (a) Into which two forms of energy is electrical energy changed by a normal lamp? (2)

    (b) If a lamp is more efficient, which of the energy forms is likely to be reduced? (1)

6.36 A cord is wrapped round the axle of a dynamo/generator on a bench. A mass is tied to the cord and allowed to fall. The dynamo is connected to a lamp that lights as the mass is falling. List the energy changes taking place as the mass falls. (6)

6.37 Body temperature is 37°C and room temperature is 20°C. A cup of tea is 60°C. Why does a warm cup of tea feel cold to drink when it has been standing for about 15 minutes? (3)

★ Make sure you know

- ★ The difference between mass and weight.
- ★ How to measure the volume of different objects and substances.
- ★ How to calculate the density of different substances.
- ★ The main features of electric circuits and their different components.
- ★ The effects of forces and motion.
- ★ The main features of light rays, including what happens to light during reflection and refraction.
- ★ The main features of sound waves, including loudness and pitch.
- ★ The effects of the Moon and the Sun on the Earth.
- ★ The main features of the different forms of energy.
- ★ How electricity is generated.

Revision tip
Use the glossary at the back of the book for definitions of key words.

Make sure you can answer the following questions. The answers are at the back of the book.

1 Suggest what apparatus and units you would use to measure the following:

   (a) The height of a Bunsen burner.

   (b) The mass of an apple.

   (c) The volume of a wooden pencil box.

   (d) The volume of water left in your water bottle.

   (e) The volume of a small bunch of keys.

2 How many boxes of drawing pins, each measuring 2 cm × 3 cm × 0.5 cm, can you fit into a box measuring 60 cm × 30 cm × 15 cm?

3 The density of water is 1 g/cm³. What is the mass of water in a box that measures 30 cm × 50 cm × 20 cm?

4 Draw a circuit that has one cell and one switch, which will light two lamps to 'normal' brightness.

5 Write down the equation used to calculate the weight of a body. Include all units.

6 A spring is 6 cm long. When a load of 100 g is attached to it, the new length is 8 cm. It returns to 6 cm when the load is removed. What will be the length when:

   (a) A load of 50 g is attached?

   (b) A load of 75 g is attached?

7 Write down two features of a lever.

8 A ray of light hits a mirror at an angle.

   (a) What is the name of this ray?

   (b) What happens to it after it has hit the mirror?

   (c) What is this process called?

9 Draw a diagram to show how you would split a ray of light that was a mixture of red and blue light, into its separate colours.

10 Complete the following table:

Season	Height of Sun	Temperature of Earth's surface	Length of shadow	Length of day
Summer				
Winter				

11 Put in ascending order of size:

   star   universe   planet   solar system   galaxy

12 What is energy?

13 List five different forms of energy.

Exam-style question answers

Chapter 1, page 2

1.1 Cannot (i) reproduce, or (ii) grow. (2)

1.2 Opening and closing of petals; flower heads following the path of the Sun. (1)

1.3 To make sure that when an organism dies, there is another similar one to replace it. (1)

1.4 An increase in the size and/or number of cells and is achieved by using the raw materials obtained through nutrition. (2)

1.5 (4)

1. Flower
2. Leaf
3. Stem
4. Root

1.6 (7)

1. Lungs
2. Liver
3. Kidneys
4. Brain
5. Heart
6. Stomach
7. Intestine

1.7 The development of special features that enable an organism to survive in a particular environment. Example: a polar bear will have a very thick coat to help it withstand the low arctic temperatures. Pine needles on trees help reduce loss of water through evaporation. (2)

1.8

Type of tooth	Function
Canine (1)	Tearing of food and/or killing (1)
Incisor (1)	Cutting and biting of food (1)
Pre-molar (1)	Tearing and grinding of food (1)
Molar (1)	Crushing and grinding of food (1)

1.9 (a) Bacteria in plaque change sugar in food into acid. The acid eats through the enamel, causing decay. (1)

(b) Any three from: regular brushing; less sugar in diet; fluoride in toothpaste or water; regular dental visits. (3)

1.10 More energy is required so more food and oxygen is needed by the cells.

Lungs breathe faster so more oxygen can pass into the blood and the heart beats faster to take this extra oxygen and food to the cells. (2)

1.11 (a) The pulse rate would rise from normal at A to possibly much higher at B. (1)

(b) The pulse rate at C will be lower than that at B, but not yet down to the normal level at A. (2)

1.12 support, protection, movement (3)

1.13 (a) Needed to combine with food to release energy for life processes. (1)

(b) Needed to combine with water to make food during photosynthesis. (1)

1.14

Factor	Why the factor is important to healthy plant growth
Air	Supply of oxygen and carbon dioxide (1)
Light	Energy supply to make photosynthesis happen (1)
Warmth	Right temperature to make all the chemical reactions in the plant happen at a satisfactory rate (1)
Water	Raw material for photosynthesis; essential to maintain healthy, firm cells (1)
Minerals	Needed to combine with food, to make plant structures (1)

1.15 (a) Because muscles *never* push. One muscle from the pair contracts, pulling the bone in a certain direction, while the opposite muscle relaxes. The reverse happens to move the bone back to where it was. (2)

(b) biceps and triceps (move the lower arm) (1)

(c) antagonistic muscles (1)

1.16 (a) To protect the brain from physical knocks. (1)

(b) To protect the spinal cord. (1)

(c) To protect the heart and lungs; to make the lungs bigger and smaller during breathing. (1)

1.17 See diagram on page 11. (5)

1.18 (a) Both are arthropods.

(b) Spider has 8 legs, but fly has 6; spider has 2 body parts, but fly has 3; spider has no antennae, but a fly does. (2)

1.19

Invertebrate (no backbone)	Vertebrate (backbone)
Octopus (1)	Cat (1)
Spider (1)	Shark (1)
Crab (1)	Frog (1)
Beetle (1)	Fox (1)

1.20 Lizard has a dry skin with scales; newt has a moist, smooth skin. (2)

1.21 Any three from:
- loss of agricultural land
- large-scale reduction of tropical rainforests
- reduction of fish stocks
- pollution of the air. (3)

1.22 Any three from:
- national parks, wildlife centres, zoos
- protection of 'endangered species'
- more efficient engines to reduce harmful emissions when burning fossil fuels
- greater awareness of using 'alternative' forms of energy (wind, geothermal) to reduce pollution from burning of fossil fuels
- recycling of household waste to reduce landfill. (3)

1.23 (a) Any two from: coal, oil, gas. (2)

(b) They pollute the air, causing acid rain. (2)

1.24 (a) D   (b) D   (c) A   (d) C   (e) B (5)

Chapter 2, page 17

2.1 No. Root cells underground receive no light and do not carry out photosynthesis. (2)

2.2 (a) (2)

Sperm   Ovum

(b) The sperm has a tail for swimming. The egg cell is larger as it contains food for the developing embryo after fertilisation. It is also not mobile. (2)

(c) The sperm cell swims to the egg, and fertilisation takes place when the male nucleus of the sperm fuses with the nucleus of the female egg to form a zygote. (2)

2.3

Name of system	What it does	Main organs in the system
Locomotion	Supports the body and allows movement (1)	Muscles and skeleton of bones (1)
Transport	Takes food to all parts of body and removes waste from them (1)	Heart and blood vessels (1)
Respiratory	Provides oxygen and removes carbon dioxide from body (1)	Windpipe and lungs (1)
Digestive	Breaks down food and absorbs useful chemicals into the blood (1)	Gut, stomach, intestine, liver (1)
Reproductive	Produces/receives gametes for next generation (1)	Testes, ovaries, uterus (1)

2.4 (a) either bread, bacon, butter or orange juice (1)

   (b) bacon and egg (2)

   (c) (i) sugar; (ii) starch. (2)

   (d) Any two from: water, vitamins, minerals, fibre (2)

2.5 At 18, protein will be required mainly for growth. At 45, growth is completed, so protein is required for repair and replacement of worn-out cells. (4)

2.6 (a) (i) Y

      (ii) Although it is mainly indigestible, it provides bulk to enable food to pass through the digestive system more efficiently. (2)

   (b) (i) X

      (ii) Contains more carbohydrate for quick energy release and therefore a greater supply of energy for the activity to come. (2)

2.7 Vitamins:

   • vitamin C: tissue repair, resistance to disease, e.g. scurvy (bleeding gums) (2)

   Minerals:

   • calcium: making of bones and teeth

   • iron: making of red blood cells (2)

2.8 (a) The chemical reactions that release energy from foods. (2)

   (b) in every living cell (1)

2.9 (a) glucose + oxygen → carbon dioxide + water + energy (6)

   (b) That air (oxygen) is required for the reaction to take place. (1)

2.10 (a) in the air sacs (1)

   (b) (i) Oxygen moves from the lungs into the bloodstream.

      (ii) Carbon dioxide moves from the bloodstream into the lungs. (1)

2.11 It is the *proportions* of carbon dioxide and oxygen that change, while the nitrogen content, which plays no part in respiration, remains the same. (2)

2.12 • Nicotine: damages blood vessels, leading to increase of blood pressure and risk of heart disease. It also causes addiction. (2)

   • Tar: causes lung cancer and blocks the action of cilia that sweep away dust and microbes. (2)

   • Carbon monoxide: reduces supply of oxygen to the cells and contributes to disease of the heart and arteries. (2)

2.13 (a) Very overweight, largely because of excess fat in the body. (2)

   (b) A combination of over-eating fatty and sugary foods, together with very little exercise. (2)

   (c) More energy is required to move heavy parts of the body, so more work has to be done by the heart to pump the extra blood to the cells to achieve this. Extra weight can cause damage to joints. (2)

2.14 512 (the number doubles every 20 minutes). (2)

2.15 (a) in the oviduct (fallopian tube) (1)

   (b) (i) The wall breaks down and passes out of the vagina. (1)

       (ii) menstruation or 'having a period' (1)

       (iii) menstrual cycle (1)

       (iv) 28 days (1)

2.16 (a) either carbon dioxide or (nitrogenous) waste, e.g. urea (1)

   (b) oxygen and food (2)

2.17 The mother may have an entirely different blood group from the fetus – these must never mix. The mother's blood pressure will be much higher than that of the fetus. (2)

2.18 Any two from:

- carried inside the body

- protected by the thick walls of the uterus

- surrounded by protective fluid contained within the amniotic sac. (2)

2.19 (a) anthers

   (b) ovules

   (c) pollination

   (d) fertilisation

   (e) fruits

   (f) germinate

   (g) grow (7)

2.20 (a) Any one from: attractive smell; display of bright/large petals. (1)

   (b) Pollen grains stick to the top of the stigma. Each pollen grain grows a tube down the style towards the ovary.

       When the pollen tube reaches the ovule, the male sex cell can combine with the female sex cell in the ovule. (3)

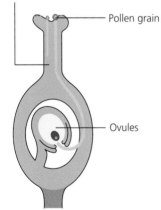

Pollen grain

Ovules

2.21 (a) 2 and 3 (2)

   (b) No; there is germination in 2, which is in the dark. (2)

   (c) That oxygen is needed for germination to take place. (1)

2.22

$$\text{carbon dioxide} + \text{water} \xrightarrow[\text{chlorophyll}]{\text{light energy}} \text{glucose} + \text{oxygen}$$ (3)

2.23 (a) chlorophyll (1)

(b) green (1)

(c) In the chloroplasts located in the cytoplasm of nearly every leaf and stem cell. (1)

(d) In the root, as photosynthesis cannot happen underground where there is no light. (1)

2.24 (a) iodine solution (1)

(b) The brown liquid turns blue/black if starch is present. (1)

(c) In good light (daytime), glucose is made at a faster rate than that at which it can be transported away, so this excess glucose is changed into starch. (1)

2.25 They are placed in different kingdoms because of the way they feed. Grass will make its own supply of sugar for respiration by photosynthesis, so it will be placed in the plant kingdom. Rabbits will eat and digest grass using the resulting sugar for respiration, so they will be placed in the animal kingdom. Mushrooms obtain their energy from the remains of dead organisms in the soil. They have no chloroplasts and do not carry out photosynthesis, so they will be placed in the fungi kingdom. (3)

2.26 These are continuous variations and they result from a combination of inherited genes and the environment, i.e. lifestyle in terms of food intake and exercise. (2)

Chapter 3, page 52

3.1 (a) flexibility: e.g. fabrics and metal wire (2)

(b) conductivity: e.g. all metals (2)

(c) hardness: e.g. diamond, steel tools and plastic safety helmets (2)

(d) strength: e.g. concrete for buildings, steel and fibreglass for boats (2)

3.2 weathering (1)

3.3 (a) Large particles with big spaces between them; good drainage; hardly ever become waterlogged. (1)

(b) Very small particles with tiny spaces between them; poor drainage; often becomes waterlogged. (1)

3.4 • solid: fixed mass, volume and shape

• liquid: fixed mass and volume but changes shape

• gas: fixed mass, but changes volume and shape (6)

3.5 (a) Solids: (i) Held strongly and closely in fixed positions. (ii) Vibrations in their fixed positions. (2)

(b) Liquids: (i) Close together but free to move around each other. (ii) Constantly moving around each other and to other places as liquid flows. (2)

(c) Gases: (i) Far apart with no forces of attraction between them. (ii) Move quickly in all directions. (2)

3.6 (a) melting (1)

   (b) evaporation (1)

   (c) freezing (1)

   (d) condensation (1)

3.7 Any two from:

   • Substances do not change into other substances – no chemical reaction.
   • May change state.
   • Changes are temporary and may be reversed. (2)

3.8 (a) Boiling point is raised well above 100°C. (1)

   (b) To stop wet roads becoming icy as salt water freezes well below 0°C. (2)

3.9 (a) oxygen and water (2)

   (b) Any three from: covering iron with a layer of oil, zinc (galvanising), paint, plastic or tin. (3)

   (c) Changes a strong useful solid into a weak useless powder. (2)

3.10 (a) coal, oil and natural gas (3)

   (b) oil and natural gas (3)

   (c) oxygen and heat (2)

   (d) Causes pollution of the air by releasing ash (smoke) and gases (carbon dioxide – greenhouse gas and/or sulfur dioxide – acid rain) into the atmosphere. (2)

3.11 (a) Soluble: able to dissolve in a solvent to form a solution. Insoluble: not able to dissolve in a solvent. (2)

   (b) The sulfur remains as a yellow solid (usually floating on top of the mixture); the copper sulfate dissolves in water to form a blue solution. (2)

   (c) (i) sulfur; (ii) copper sulfate solution (2)

3.12 The missing words are as follows:

   (a) solids; different (2)

   (b) insoluble; liquids (2)

   (c) sink (1)

   (d) decanting (1)

3.13 (a) solvent (1)

   (b) evaporated; solute (2)

Chapter 4, page 64

4.1

Elements	Compounds	Mixtures
Carbon (1)	Carbon dioxide (1)	Air (1)
Iron filings (1)	Distilled water (1)	Sea water (1)
Magnesium (1)	Sodium chloride (1)	Crude oil (1)
Oxygen (1)	Iron sulfide (1)	Dilute sulfuric acid (1)

4.2

Metal element	Non-metal element	Compound
Iron filings (1)	Carbon (1)	Copper sulfate (1)
Magnesium (1)	Oxygen (1)	Water (1)
Mercury (1)	Sulfur (1)	Zinc oxide (1)
Sodium (1)		

4.3 **(a)** Mercury: the only one of these metals that is a liquid at room temperature. (2)

(b) Sodium: the only one of these metals that reacts with oxygen to form a base that is soluble in water, producing an alkali. The other oxides are insoluble in water. (2)
or
Iron: the only metal that will rust. (2)

(c) Copper oxide: the only one of these oxides that is a solid and a base that neutralises acids. The others are gases, which dissolve in water to form acids. (2)

(d) Sulfur: the only one that does not conduct electricity. (2)

4.4 Heating: adding energy to a substance to raise its temperature. (1)

Chemical reaction: rearranging elements to form completely new substances. (1)

Reactant: the substance you start with before a chemical reaction. (1)

Decompose: the splitting up of the substance into products, caused by a chemical reaction. (1)

Products: the substances produced as a result of a chemical reaction. (1)

4.5 **(a)** There will be an increase in mass during the reaction as reactants combine to form products. (2)

(b) For example: (5)

magnesium (s) + oxygen (g) → magnesium oxide (s)

Magnesium has combined with oxygen from the air during burning to form magnesium oxide. This has more mass because of the extra oxygen that has combined with the magnesium.

4.6 **(a) (i)** A – nitrogen

(ii) B – oxygen (1)

(b) Any one from: carbon dioxide, noble gases (argon, krypton, helium, neon). (1)

(c) (i) water vapour (1)

(ii) Either white anhydrous copper sulfate turns blue or blue cobalt chloride turns pink. (2)

4.7

Process	Nitrogen	Oxygen	Carbon dioxide
Burning a fossil fuel	Same (1)	Decrease (1)	Increase (1)
Photosynthesis	Same (1)	Increase (1)	Decrease (1)
Respiration	Same (1)	Decrease (1)	Increase (1)
Passing air through limewater	Same (1)	Same (1)	Decrease (1)
Rusting	Same (1)	Decrease (1)	Same (1)

4.8 **(a)** See diagram on page 71. (6)

(b) See if it boils at 100°C – if it does, it is pure. (2)

4.9 (a) evaporation (1)

(b) filtration (1)

(c) chromatography (1)

4.10 hydrochloric acid – red (1)

limewater – stays blue (1)

sodium hydroxide – stays blue (1)

sugar solution – stays blue (1)

water – stays blue (1)

4.11 pH scale (a scale of numbers ranging from 1 to 14). (5)

pH scale (a scale of numbers ranging from 1 to 14)

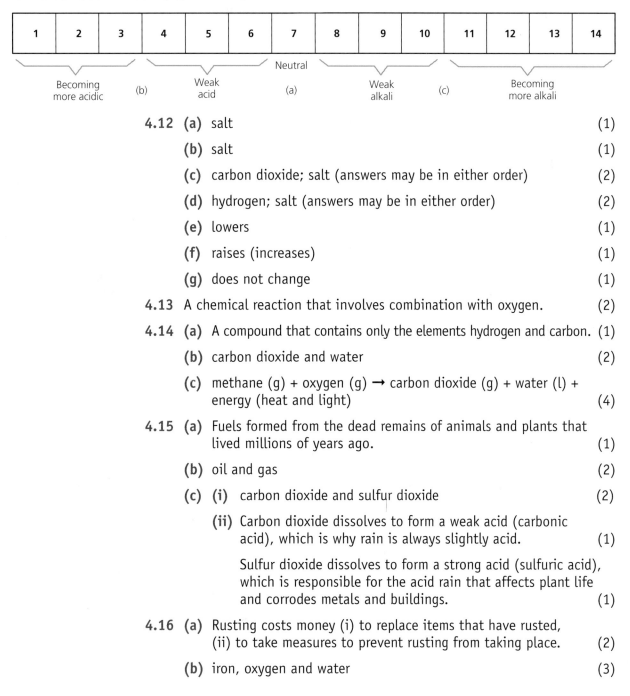

4.12 (a) salt (1)

(b) salt (1)

(c) carbon dioxide; salt (answers may be in either order) (2)

(d) hydrogen; salt (answers may be in either order) (2)

(e) lowers (1)

(f) raises (increases) (1)

(g) does not change (1)

4.13 A chemical reaction that involves combination with oxygen. (2)

4.14 (a) A compound that contains only the elements hydrogen and carbon. (1)

(b) carbon dioxide and water (2)

(c) methane (g) + oxygen (g) → carbon dioxide (g) + water (l) + energy (heat and light) (4)

4.15 (a) Fuels formed from the dead remains of animals and plants that lived millions of years ago. (1)

(b) oil and gas (2)

(c) (i) carbon dioxide and sulfur dioxide (2)

(ii) Carbon dioxide dissolves to form a weak acid (carbonic acid), which is why rain is always slightly acid. (1)

Sulfur dioxide dissolves to form a strong acid (sulfuric acid), which is responsible for the acid rain that affects plant life and corrodes metals and buildings. (1)

4.16 (a) Rusting costs money (i) to replace items that have rusted, (ii) to take measures to prevent rusting from taking place. (2)

(b) iron, oxygen and water (3)

(c) By covering the iron with a layer of grease, oil, paint or plastic. (1)

By covering the iron with a less reactive metal, e.g. tin. (1)

By coating iron with a layer of zinc (i.e. galvanising). This is known as sacrificial protection. (1)

4.17 Metals are placed in order according to how well they react with oxygen, water, steam and acids in what is called the reactivity series. (1)

4.18 oxidation: combining with oxygen (2)

reduction: removal of oxygen from a compound by another substance (2)

4.19 (a) zinc + magnesium oxide → no reaction (2)

(b) zinc + copper oxide → zinc oxide + copper (2)

(c) magnesium + iron oxide → magnesium oxide + iron (2)

(d) iron + copper sulfate → iron sulfate + copper (2)

(e) iron + magnesium sulfate → no reaction (2)

(f) zinc + iron sulfate → zinc sulfate + iron (2)

4.20 D, B, C, A (most reactive first) (4)

4.21 (a) (i) copper oxide (1)

(ii) copper oxide + carbon → carbon dioxide + copper (4)

(b) (i) raise the pH (1)

(ii) an iron nail (1)

4.22 iron oxide + carbon → iron + carbon dioxide (4)

4.23 Iron is higher than copper in the reactivity series and is harder to extract, i.e. far greater temperatures than those produced by a charcoal fire are needed. Iron was only able to be extracted when the technology for creating more heat from better furnaces had been developed. (3)

4.24 (a) lead sulfide (galena) + oxygen + heat → lead oxide + sulfur dioxide (5)

(b) lead oxide + carbon + heat → lead + carbon dioxide (5)

(c) Yes. Iron is higher than lead in the reactivity series. (2)

4.25 (a) iron ore: the source of iron. (2)

limestone: to turn sandy rock into slag (2)

coke: a supply of carbon to react with iron oxide (2)

(b) carbon monoxide (1)

(c) iron oxide + carbon monoxide → iron + carbon dioxide (4)

4.26 (a) gold, iron, aluminium (3)

(b) Aluminium requires large quantities of electricity to extract it from its ore. This, and the high temperatures required, make it a much more expensive process than the extraction of iron. (2)

(c) Gold is a rare metal, found in small quantities. (2)

Chapter 5, page 88

5.1 **(a)** normal brightness (1)

(b) bright (1)

(c) dim (1)

5.2 **(a)** (3)

(b) They will be equally dim. (1)

(c) **(i)** There is a gap in the circuit. (1)

(ii) One/more of the lamps might be broken. (1)

(iii) One of the cells is the wrong way round. (1)

5.3 Current always takes the easiest route, which may not always be the shortest route. (2)

5.4 Any four from:

- Make a stationary object move.

- Make a moving object go faster or slower.

- Make a moving object change direction.

- Make a moving object stop.

- Change the shape of an object. (4)

5.5 weight of the boat (downwards); upthrust by water (upwards) (2)

5.6 When a force acts, the other force of the pair acting in the opposite direction is called the reaction force. (1)

5.7 **(a)** Materials that are attracted by a magnet are said to be magnetic. (1)

(b) The end of a magnet that points towards the magnetic north pole is called the north-seeking pole. (1)

(c) Unlike poles attract; like poles repel. (2)

5.8 **(a)** weight (1)

(b) Downwards towards the Earth's centre. (1)

5.9 **(a)** A force that opposes motion. (1)

(b) When two substances rub together. (1)

5.10 Any four from:

- Tyres and road: useful for grip, movement and control of direction – help.

- Shape of cyclist: air resistance slows movement, so speed cyclists will crouch to be as streamlined as possible – nuisance.

- Gears and chain: friction adds to the effort needed to turn these – nuisance.

- Brakes: enable the cycle to be stopped – help.
- Rubber on handlebar grips: make it easier to hold on – help. (8)

5.11 Light from a luminous source reflects off the table into our eyes. (2)

5.12 **(a)** transparent (1)

(b) opaque (1)

(c) translucent (1)

5.13 It bounces off the surface at the same angle as it hits the mirror surface. This is called reflection. (2)

5.14 by vibrations (2)

5.15 **(a)** Pluck it to start it vibrating. (2)

(b) Tighten the string or make it shorter. (2)

(c) Pluck it harder to make bigger vibrations. (1)

5.16 Space is said to be a vacuum and sound is not able to travel through a vacuum because there are no particles to squash or stretch. (2)

5.17 The Earth spins on its axis, completing one turn every 24 hours. During this time, half of the Earth faces the Sun – daytime – while the other half is in darkness – night-time. (1)

5.18 the spinning of the Earth (1)

5.19 Midday – Sun is high in the sky and shadows are shortest. (1)

Evening – Sun is low in the sky and shadows are long. (1)

5.20 27 days – this is the time it takes for the Moon to orbit the Earth. (2)

5.21 The Moon is not a light source and it is hard to see during daytime. We see it best at night because light from the Sun is reflected from it. (2)

Chapter 6, page 100

6.1 mass and volume (2)

6.2 $\text{density} = \dfrac{\text{mass}}{\text{volume}}$ (3)

6.3 **(a)** A = 7.5 g/cm³ (2)

(b) B = 11.0 g/cm³ (2)

(c) C = 2.7 g/cm³ (2)

(d) D = 2.7 g/cm³ (2)

6.4 C and D are the same material. They have the same density. (2)

6.5 glass (volume 1071 cm³; volume of marble 937 cm³). (1)

6.6 234 000 g or 234 kg (m should be converted to cm when calculating the volume of the room) (2)

6.7 **(a)** (4)

(b) The ammeter reading goes down. (1)

(c) It must be connected the right way round, i.e. positive to positive. (1)

6.8 (a) (i) A

(ii) A and B (2)

(b) (i) A and B

(ii) A and C (2)

6.9 (a) No. Once a fuse 'blows', the circuit is broken immediately, so the second fuse is not needed. (2)

(b) When there is a current in a circuit that is too high for the fuse, the fuse wire heats, melts and breaks the circuit, stopping all current in the circuit immediately. (2)

(c) To protect components from currents that are too large and might well damage them. (2)

6.10 (a) Wrap the insulated wire around the iron nail and connect each end of the wire to a battery or cell. (3)

(b) Bring a magnet close to the nail. If there is repulsion between the two, then the nail has become a magnet. (2)

(c) Either increase the number of turns of wire or increase the current by adding another battery or more cells. (2)

6.11 (a) an AND circuit (there are two switches: one on the lamp and one on the socket) (1)

(b) (9)

Inputs		Output
A	B	Q
0	0	0
0	1	0
1	0	0
1	1	1

6.12 (a) 30 N (2)

(b) 300 N (2)

(c) 1800 N (2)

(d) 5 N (2)

(e) 3.2 N (2)

6.13 (a) 40 kg (2)

(b) 400 N (2)

(c) 64 N (2)

6.14 (a) increase; accelerate (2)

(b) decrease (1)

(c) constant speed (1)

6.15 (a) 48 cm (2)

(b) 4 cm (2)

6.16 45 Nm (TM = 300 N × 0.15 m) or 4500 Ncm (TM = 300 N × 15 cm) (2)

6.17 10 N (2)

6.18 360 cm away from the pivot (2)

6.19 **(a)** $6\,N/cm^2$ (2)

    (b) $5\,N/cm^2$ (2)

    (c) $1000\,N/cm^2$ (2)

6.20 $4\,cm^2$ (2)

6.21 Any three from:

- They are very fast.
- They travel in straight lines.
- They will not travel through opaque materials, so forming shadows.
- They can be absorbed. (3)

6.22 **(a)** The bending of a light ray. (1)

    (b) At the boundary between two different materials through which a light ray is passing. (1)

    (c) Light changes speed as it passes through materials that have different densities. (1)

6.23 **(a)** (1)

mirror — light ray from a hidden object — reflected light ray — obstacle, such as a wall or hedge — viewer — mirror

    (b) a periscope (1)

6.24 3000 m or 3 km (2)

6.25 3.3 s (2)

6.26 **(a)** **(i)** frequency

        (ii) amplitude (2)

    (b) The high, loud note has higher frequency and larger amplitude than the low, quiet note. (2)

6.27 The Earth is tilted on its axis, making part of it closer to the Sun. (2)

6.28 **(a)** Earth; Sun (2)

    (b) Moon; Earth (2)

6.29 The distance that light travels in 1 year. (1)

6.30 Because light from the stars does not have to pass though the Earth's atmosphere, which would absorb some of the light, reducing the quality of the pictures. (2)

6.31 (a) Work is done when (i) a force produces motion; (ii) when something is heated. (1)

(b) joule (J) (1)

(c) amount of work done (J) = amount of energy supplied (J) (2)

6.32 When energy changes form: total amount of energy at the start = total amount of energy at the end. (2)

6.33

Form of energy at start	Component	Form(s) of energy at end
Electrical	Lamp (1)	Light, heat (1)
Chemical (1)	Cell	Electrical, heat
Chemical	Bunsen burner	Light, sound, heat (3)
Sound	Microphone	Electrical, heat (1)
Electrical (1)	Loudspeaker	Sound, heat
Electrical	Motor	Kinetic, sound, heat (1)
Kinetic (1)	Dynamo/generator	Electrical, sound, heat
Light	Solar cell (1)	Electrical, heat

6.34 (a) Fuels formed from the fossilised remains of animals and plants that lived over many millions of years ago. (2)

(b) Any two from: coal, oil and gas. (2)

(c) Once burned, they cannot be used again and we are using them up faster than they can be replaced (if at all). (2)

(d) No. Fossil fuels provide raw materials for the manufacture of plastics, medicines, cosmetics and synthetic fibres. (2)

6.35 (a) light and heat (2)

(b) heat (1)

6.36 (6)

gravitational potential energy → kinetic energy → electrical energy + sound energy + light energy + heat

6.37 The cup of tea cools to room temperature (20°C). The tea, now at 20°C, is put into your mouth, which is at 37°C. Heat will flow out from your mouth to the tea, so the tea will feel cold. (3)

Test yourself answers

Chapter 1, page 2

1 any living thing

2 (a) nutrition, movement, reproduction, growth

  (b) Nutrition: obtain and absorb food.

   Movement: change of place and/or position.

   Reproduction: an organism making more of its own kind.

   Growth: becoming bigger by increasing size and/or number of cells.

3 (a) Pumps blood around the body.

  (b) Take blood away from the heart to the body.

  (c) Take blood towards the heart from the body.

4 Any two from: jointed limbs (in pairs); hard outer bodies (exoskeleton); segmented bodies.

5 (a) The place where an organism lives.

  (b) The sum of all biological (e.g. other animals and plants), chemical (e.g. pH, salinity of water) and physical (e.g. light, temperature) factors that affect an organism.

Chapter 2, page 17

1

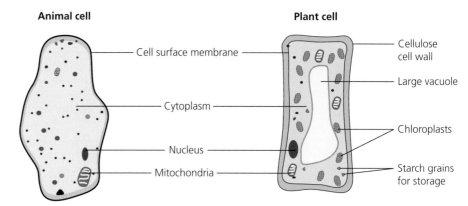

2 Tissue: specialised cells of the same type combined together, e.g. muscles, skin layers.

Organ: a structure made from various tissues that performs a specific function, e.g. eye, leaf, carpel.

System: a collection of combined organs that enable a specific job to be done, e.g. reproductive system.

3   (a) (i) Carbohydrate (although fats provide a storage of energy for use when supplies of carbohydrate become low).

        (ii) sugar – fruits, jams, sweets, soft drinks; starch – potatoes, flour products, nuts

    (b) (i) protein

        (ii) meats, fish, milk, cheese, eggs, nuts

4   (a) adolescence

    (b) sperm cell; testis or testes

    (c) egg cell or ovum; ovary or ovaries

    (d) zygote

    (e) implantation

    (f) pregnant

5   Any two from:

    • Exercise causes the heart to beat faster, which keeps it healthy.

    • Exercise develops muscles.

    • Exercise reduces the amount of stored fat in the body.

6   The manufacture of food by a plant using light energy from the Sun.

7   carbon dioxide and water

8   glucose (sugar) and oxygen

9   Some of this will be used by the plant itself, for respiration. Oxygen not used by the plant will be released through the stomata.

10 It is used for respiration, which is needed by every living cell. The leaves make more glucose than they need, so glucose is transported to other parts of the plant for respiration.

    It is also used for making living material – increasing biomass.

    In order to grow, plants need a constant supply of proteins, chlorophyll and fats, which can be made from sugars such as glucose.

11 (a) As soluble salts dissolved in the water in the soil around the plants roots.

    (b) Numerous thin-walled root hair cells that absorb water and soluble salts.

        The great number of root hair cells increases surface area and the thin cell walls enable water and minerals to be taken into the plant more efficiently.

12 The differences between organisms of the same species.

13 Any one from: colour of eyes/hair; blood group; male/female; freckles or the shape of the face. These are features that result from the inheritance of genes from the parents.

14 Sorting organisms with similar characteristics (features) into groups.

15 Both are vertebrates and belong to the class Mammals. Both are warm-blooded, have skins that are partially covered with hair or fur. Both will have been born alive and fed on milk from the mother's mammary glands.

16 Jointed limbs in pairs; hard outer covering (exoskeleton); bodies divided into segments (compartments).

17

Vertebrate	Invertebrate
Emu	Earthworm
Shark	Spider
Whale	Crab
Frog	Beetle
Turtle	
Fox	

18 An ecosystem is a habitat (the place) together with all the organisms living within that habitat.

19 This describes the conditions within an ecosystem.

20 This refers to the numbers of organisms of the same species that exist in a habitat.

21 Food shortage; shortage of space; increase of toxins (poisons); predation.

22 (a) Rose. It is the only organism in the chain that can make its own food – using photosynthesis. It is the primary source of food in the chain.

(b) Any two from:

• Aphids die out – killed by insecticide.

• Rose grows better – not being eaten by aphids.

• Robin and cat might move away – a supply of food has disappeared.

23 (a) A food web is a set of interconnected food chains.

(b) In a food web, consumers have more than one supply of food, unlike a food chain, where there is only one supply of food.

Chapter 3, page 52

1 (a) These are specific to substances and may be observed and/or measured without the substances changing into another substance.

(b) The composition of a substance and how it changes into another substance. When this happens, a chemical reaction has taken place.

2 Decayed animal and plant remains that add nutrients and help keep soil moist.

3 (a) C – solid

(b) B – liquid

(c) A – gas

4 New substances are made as a result of a chemical reaction.

Change is permanent and cannot be reversed.

5   (a) ink

(b) water

(c) blue powder

Chapter 4, page 64

1   (a) A single substance that forms the building blocks of all matter.

(b) 100

(c) in the periodic table

(d) The atoms of any particular element are all the same.

2   All elements present as reactants will also be present in the product(s) of a chemical reaction.

total mass of reactant(s) = total mass of product(s)

3   (a) Changes in appearance to indicate the presence of particular substances.

(b) Any four from:

• Limewater: to test for presence of carbon dioxide.

• Anhydrous copper sulfate: to test for presence of water.

• Litmus: to test for presence of acids/alkalis.

• Universal indicator: to test for the presence and strength of acids/alkalis.

4   (a) hydrochloric acid: stays red

(b) limewater: turns blue

(c) sodium hydroxide: turns blue

(d) sugar solution: stays red

(e) water: stays red

5   Oxygen is the only colourless gas that re-lights a glowing splint.

6   (a) carbon (s) + oxygen (g) → carbon dioxide (g)

(b) magnesium (s) + oxygen (g) → magnesium oxide (s)

(c) sulfur (s) + oxygen (g) → sulfur dioxide (g)

7   (a) copper sulfate + iron → iron sulfate + copper

(b) silver nitrate + copper → copper nitrate + silver

8   A substance that is a mixture of a metal compound and rock.

9   (a) Plastic: light and does not break.

(b) Copper: a very good conductor of electricity; flexible as thin wires.

(c) Plastic: easy to shape and does not rust; does not need painting regularly.

(d) Iron: strong and will not melt at the temperature of hot ash.

(e) Aluminium: strong and light (low density).

1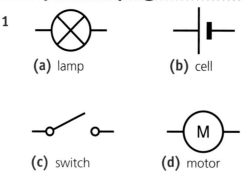

(a) lamp (b) cell

(c) switch (d) motor

2 Components are connected together one after the other in a single path.

3 a push or pull

4 newton (N)

5 a newton meter (newton spring balance)

6 a force of attraction between any two bodies

7 Push – gravity only pulls.

8 Any three from: Sun, stars, lamps, television sets, flames.

9 Light travels in straight lines.

Light travels very fast.

10 (a) 365¼ days

(b) 1 year

11 A moon orbits a planet. A planet orbits a star.

Chapter 6, page 100

1 (a) A ruler marked in cm.

(b) A balance (scales) marked in g.

(c) A ruler marked in cm. Measure lengths and multiply to find volume in cm^3.

(d) A measuring cylinder marked in cm^3. Pour water from water bottle into the cylinder and read off the volume.

(e) A measuring cylinder with some water in it. Measure the volume of water that the keys displace in cm^3.

2 9000

3 30 000 g (or 30 kg)

4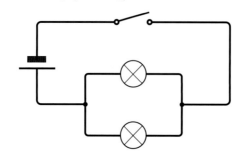

5 weight (N) = mass (kg) × gravitational force (N/kg)

6 (a) 7 cm

(b) 7.5 cm

7 Has a rigid body.

Able to turn about a pivot.

8 (a) incident ray

(b) It bounces off at the same angle.

(c) reflection

9

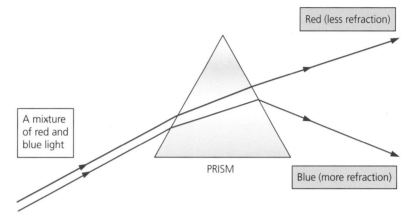

10

Season	Height of Sun	Temperature of Earth's surface	Length of shadow	Length of day
Summer	High	Warm	Short	Long
Winter	Low	Cold	Long	Short

11 planet; star; solar system; galaxy; universe

12 Energy is a measure of (i) work that has been done, or (ii) work that is able to be done.

13 Any five from:

- kinetic energy
- gravitational potential energy
- elastic (strain) energy
- chemical energy
- electrical energy
- thermal energy
- light energy
- sound energy
- nuclear energy

Glossary

Biology

Aerobic respiration	The form of respiration involving air.
Antagonistic muscles	A pair of muscles that have opposite actions enabling movement to take place.
Anther	Part of the stamen, the male part of a flower.
Arteries	Blood vessels that carry blood away from the heart.
Arthropods	The class of animal that has jointed limbs, a hard outer body covering and segmented body.
Bacteria	Cells that live and grow outside living cells.
Brain	An organ found in the head that controls many of the life processes in animals.
Canines	Killing teeth that are well developed in carnivores.
Carbohydrate	A food substance, including starches and sugars, which supplies most of the energy we need.
Carbon cycle	A series of chemical reactions that follow what happens to carbon, carbon dioxide, oxygen, water and sugars in the environment – it links photosynthesis, respiration and decay.
Carnivore	An animal that eats other animals.
Carpel	The female part of a flower – made up of stigma, style and ovary.
Cell surface membrane	The part of a cell surrounding the cytoplasm.
Chlorophyll	A green pigment (colour) in plant cells that can absorb light energy in photosynthesis.
Competition	Two or more organisms trying to obtain the same thing from their environment.
Consumer	An organism in a food chain that eats other organisms.
Cytoplasm	All of the living material of a cell, other than the nucleus.
DNA	The chemical **d**eoxyribo**n**ucleic **a**cid, which makes up the coded information in the genes in the nucleus of the cell.
Egestion	The process of removing solid waste material from the body.

Embryo root	Part of the plant seed that grows out of the seed during germination to anchor the young plant in the soil and absorb water.
Embryo shoot	Part of the plant seed that grows out of the seed during germination to form the stem and leaves.
Enzymes	Chemicals that enable other chemical reactions to happen.
Fat	A food substance providing a supply of energy.
Fertilisation	The joining together of male and female sex cells.
Fetus	A developing baby in the womb.
Fibre	A substance that comes from plants that provides bulk to our food to enable it to travel through the digestive system more efficiently.
Filament	Part of the stamen, the male part of a flower.
Flower	Part of the plant containing the reproductive organs.
Food chain/web	The passage of food energy between different living organisms – made up of producers and consumers.
Food store	Part of the plant seed that provides the first raw materials for the growth of the young plant.
Fungi	One of the five kingdoms of living organisms that has similar cells to plants but is unable to carry out photosynthesis.
Gamete	A male (sperm/pollen) or female (ovum) sex cell.
Gene	Coded information contained within the nucleus of a cell, which determines how a cell replicates itself.
Germination	The change from a seed to a young plant.
Glucose	The sugar obtained from digested food, which reacts with oxygen in respiration.
Growth	A life process where an organism increases in size and/or number of cells.
Heart	An organ that pumps blood through all parts of an animal's body.
Herbivore	An animal that eats plants.
Hibernation	A way of avoiding harsh conditions by sleeping for a long period.
Incisors	Cutting teeth in the front of the jaw.
Intestine	A long tube that runs from the stomach to the anus and breaks the food down, and where useful substances are passed into the blood.
Invertebrate	An animal that has no backbone.
Leaf	Part of the plant that traps sunlight, manufactures food and releases oxygen into the air.

Lungs	Organs that allow oxygen to enter the body and carbon dioxide to leave it.
Migration	A way of avoiding harsh conditions by moving to a new habitat.
Mineral salts	Substances that usually combine with another food to form different parts of the body, such as teeth, bones (from calcium) and red blood cells (from iron).
Molars	Teeth used for grinding located at the side of the jaw.
Nocturnal	Animals that are active at night, like an owl.
Nucleus	The control centre of a cell, containing the genetic material.
Nutrients	The food substances required to carry out the processes that are essential for life.
Nutrition	The life process that provides a living organism with its food.
Obesity	An extremely heavy body weight that often causes illness.
Omnivore	An animal that eats both plants and animals.
Ovary	Part of the carpel, the female part of a flower.
Ovule	The part of the plant's ovary that contains the egg cell.
Ovum	A cell containing the female genes.
Oxygen	The gas required by all living organisms in order to burn up food for energy.
Photosynthesis	The process carried out by plants that uses light energy to change carbon dioxide gas and water into food and oxygen.
Plaque	A sticky mixture of bacteria and sugar that often leads to tooth decay.
Pollination	The transfer of the male sex cell, the pollen grain, from the anther to the stigma of a flower.
Pre-molars	Ridged teeth that tear and grind food.
Predation	When animals hunt and capture other animals. This will affect the size of the population.
Predator	An animal that hunts, captures and often eats other animals.
Prey	An animal hunted and captured by other animals.
Protein	A food substance used in the growth and repair of cells.
Pulse	The stretching of artery walls caused by the beating of the heart.

Reproduction	The life process that produces new individual organisms.
Respiration	The release of energy for life processes.
Roots	The part of a plant that absorbs water and minerals from the soil; they also anchor the plant firmly in the soil.
Seed	What develops if an ovule is fertilised.
Single-celled organism	One of the five kingdoms of living organisms where the organism has a single cell with a nucleus.
Skeleton	The bony structure of the body (including the skull, collarbone, shoulder blade, ribcage and pelvis) that supports the tissues and organs and enables movement to take place.
Sperm	A cell containing the male genes.
Stamen	The male part of a flower made up of the filament and anther.
Stamina	The ability to keep working or exercising for a long time.
Starch	A type of carbohydrate that is stored in the muscles and liver in humans and is the food store in many plant tissues.
Stem	The part of the plant that supports the leaves, holding them up towards the light.
Stigma	The part of the carpel where the pollen grain lands; the female part of a flower.
Stomach	A part of the body that stores food; it churns and mixes the food up with chemicals, helping to break it down.
Style	A part of the carpel, the female part of a flower.
Veins	Blood vessels that carry blood towards the heart.
Vertebrate	An animal with a backbone (as part of a bony skeleton).
Viruses	Microbes that invade living cells in order to reproduce.
Vitamins	Substances needed in very small amounts to enable the body to use other nutrients more efficiently: for example vitamin C, which is crucial in avoiding bleeding gums and loose teeth.
Water	The liquid formed from a combination of hydrogen and oxygen and required by all living organisms in order to survive.
Zygote	The fertilised egg produced when gametes are joined together during fertilisation.

Chemistry

Atom	The smallest particle of an element.
Boiling	A physical change in which heat changes a liquid into a gas, e.g. liquid water into steam.
Boiling point	The temperature at which a liquid changes to a gas or a gas changes to a liquid.
Compound	A material formed from the chemical combination reaction of two or more elements.
Condensation	A physical change in which cooling a gas changes it into a liquid.
Conductor	A material that allows something to pass through it, e.g. a metal wire is a conductor because it allows electricity and/or heat to pass through it.
Decanting	A way of separating a solid from a liquid by letting the solid settle and then pouring the liquid into another container.
Decomposition	A chemical reaction in which one substance is broken down into several products.
Density	The amount of mass in a specified volume – usually the mass of 1 cm^3.
Dissolving	A process that spreads out particles of a solid through a liquid to produce a solution.
Distillation	The separation and recovery of a solvent from a solution.
Element	A material that is made up of one type of atom.
Evaporating	A physical process in which a liquid changes into a gas.
Filtrate	The liquid that passes through a filter.
Filtration	A process that uses a filter (like a sieve) to separate an insoluble solid from a liquid.
Fossil fuel	A fuel that was made millions of years ago from the bodies of dead animals and plants, e.g. coal, oil, gas.
Freezing	The physical change of a liquid into a solid as the temperature falls, e.g. liquid water changing to ice. This is also known as solidifying.
Humus	A sticky material in soil made by the decay of dead animals and plants.
Insoluble	Something that will not dissolve in a liquid, e.g. sand is insoluble in water.
Insulator	A material that does not allow heat/electricity to pass through it, e.g. polystyrene.

Litmus paper	Test papers used to detect the presence of acids or alkalis.
Loam	A soil for growing plants, with an ideal mixture of rock particles, air, water, minerals and humus.
Magnet	A substance that can attract a metal such as iron.
Melting	A physical process in which heat changes a solid to a liquid, e.g. ice can melt into liquid water.
Melting point	The temperature at which a solid changes to a liquid or a liquid changes to a solid.
Metal	A material that may be hard, can be bent, polished and conducts heat and electricity. (A material that does not have these characteristics is called a non-metal.)
Molecule	A particle made from two or more atoms joined together, as a result of a chemical reaction.
Neutralisation	A chemical reaction between acids and alkalis, producing a neutral solution.
Oxidation	A chemical reaction where elements combine with oxygen to form compounds called oxides.
Periodic table	A table of all the elements listed in order of their atomic number.
pH scale	A numbering system used to show the strengths of acids and alkalis.
Reactivity series	A list of metals showing how well they react with oxygen, water, steam and acids.
Reduction	A chemical reaction in which oxygen is taken away by another substance.
Residue	The solid material left on a filter when a mixture is poured through it.
Rusting	A process in which air (oxygen) and water cause a chemical change to iron.
Sieving	The process of using a mesh to separate a mixture of solid particles of different sizes.
Soluble	Able to dissolve in a liquid, e.g. salt is soluble in water.
Solute	A substance that can dissolve in a liquid (the solvent) to form a solution.
Solution	The mixture formed when a solute dissolves in a solvent.
Solvent	The liquid that can dissolve a solute to form a solution.
Sublimation	The change of state from solid to gas or gas to solid, missing out the liquid state.
Universal indicator	A liquid or test paper used to find the pH value of a solution, depending on the colour.
Water cycle	The change of water between solid, liquid and gas that circulates water around the planet Earth.

Physics

Air resistance	The force of friction existing between an object and the air.
AND circuit	A circuit with two switches connected in series so that the circuit will only work when both switches are on.
Attract	To pull towards each other, e.g. unlike poles of a magnet attract each other.
Cell	A source of electricity in which chemical reactions change chemical energy into electrical energy.
Chemical energy	This is energy released when a chemical reaction takes place.
Circuit	Some electrical components connected together, so that electric current can flow.
Electrical energy	The energy due to an electric current moving energy from one place to another.
Force	Something causing (i) a stationary body to move and/or change shape; (ii) change in the speed or the direction of movement of a moving body. This can be a push, pull, support (reaction) or upthrust.
Friction	A force that opposes motion between two objects when they rub together.
Gravitational potential energy	The energy that a body has because of its position and its mass; the vertical height from which the body falls and the force of gravity.
Gravity	The force that pulls objects together (for example, gravity is the force that pulls us towards the centre of the Earth and which keeps the planets in orbit around the Sun).
Joule	The unit used to measure amount of energy.
Kinetic energy	The energy that a body has when it is moving; depends upon its mass and speed.
Light energy	Energy carried by electromagnetic waves from luminous sources, e.g. from the Sun.
Light-dependent resistor	A component whose resistance will decrease with increasing light intensity.
Light-emitting diode	A component that emits light when a small current flows through it.
Loudness	A measure of the intensity of a sound – in other words, how much energy the sound has.
Luminous	Giving out light, e.g. the Sun is a luminous object.
Newton	The unit used to describe amount of force.
Opaque	Not allowing light to pass through.

OR circuit	A circuit with two switches connected in parallel so that the circuit will work when either or both are switched on.
Parallel circuits	Two or more individual circuits connected to the same electrical supply.
Pitch	How high or low a sound is.
Pivot	The point around which something turns.
Poles	The two ends of a magnet; one end will be north-seeking and the other end south-seeking.
Refraction	The bending of light as it moves from one material to another one of different density.
Repulsion	Pushing apart, e.g. like (similar) poles of a magnet repel each other.
Resistor	A component that is designed to reduce the current in a circuit.
Series circuit	A circuit with all the components connected one after another; there is no choice for the pathway of the current.
Shadow	An area behind an opaque object opposite a light source.
Sound energy	Energy carried by sound waves.
Strain (elastic potential) energy	The energy that a body has, due to how much it has been bent or stretched.
Thermal energy	The energy due to the movement of the molecules inside a substance.
Translucent	Allowing light to pass through but creating a change in the light rays so that the image is unclear.
Transparent	Allowing light to pass through without changing the light rays, so that the image is clear.
Vacuum	A space with no particles in it.
Vibration	The movement of an object backward and forward, usually at high speed – there is no sound without vibration.
Weight	The force of gravity pulling an object downwards towards the Earth's centre.